GREENSPAN'S
BUBBLES

GREENSPAN'S BUBBLES

The Age of Ignorance at the Federal Reserve

William A. Fleckenstein
with Frederick Sheehan

New York   Chicago   San Francisco   Lisbon   London
Madrid   Mexico City   Milan   New Delhi   San Juan
Seoul   Singapore   Sydney   Toronto

The **McGraw·Hill** *Companies*

1 2 3 4 5 6 7 8 9 0 DOC/DOC 0 9 8

ISBN: 978-0-07-159158-4
MHID: 0-07-159158-3

McGraw-Hill books are available at special quantity discounts to use as premiums and sales promotions, or for use in corporate training programs. To contact a representative please visit the Contact Us pages at www.mhprofessional.com.

For my girls: Melody, Jacqueline, and Nicole. And for my buddy Marc, who died way too young.

—W.A.F.

To Margaret, for both her spirit and ingenuity: of the latter, tethering Freddie to his toy box and helping Anna draw her own book.

—F.S.

CONTENTS

ACKNOWLEDGMENTS

This book could never have been written without the help of my partner in the study of the life and times of Alan Greenspan, Fred Sheehan. His tireless research efforts and knowledge of the material made this book possible. When I write "I" in this book, I mean "we," as we both feel exactly the same way about the subject. Those who want to know even more about the Chairman should look to read Fred's in-depth version, to be published some time in the future.

Writing this book would also not have been possible had my friend Molly Evans not kept diligent records of all my old columns. Her knowledge of where to find everything and her help with the charts were invaluable.

I owe special thanks to my wife, Melody, who not only put up with me during the entire process, but always kept her eye on the forest. I am also fortunate to have Jim Grant as a friend. Jim told me exactly what I needed to do to accomplish this task and he also pitched in to help me turn a phrase or two. If you read something especially well stated, chances are, Jim had a hand in it.

I'd like also to thank those friends who either read a draft and gave me valuable feedback or helped me with the data gathering: Fred Hickey, Gordy Ringeon, Gert von Der Linde, Bob Campbell, Doug Noland, John Crowl, Mary Levai, Bill Savoy, and especially, Caroline Baum.

Lastly, I'd like to thank Jeanne Glasser, my editor at McGraw-Hill, for coming up with the idea to have me write this book.

—Bill Fleckenstein

This book could never have been written if not for Bill Fleckenstein's ability to distill the abstractions of finance and bureaucratese into a vivid narrative. The clock was a stern taskmaster. Akin to an intermediate skier racing down a double-diamond slope, Bill had no time to pause and reorient his path, to stray off the trail, or to snowplow into the finish. It was also a pleasure to work with Bill, our thoughts often anticipating each others'.

I am grateful to those Bill has thanked above. My own special thanks go to the Government Documents Department of the Boston Public Library.

—Fred Sheehan

Introduction

A True Accounting: The Greenspan Era
(1987–2006)

Those who cannot remember the past are condemned to repeat it.

—*George Santayana*, The Life of Reason

A debate has emerged in this country regarding the legacy Alan Greenspan has left after his nearly 19 years as Chairman of the Federal Reserve. Some have argued that Greenspan ushered in an era of prosperity. Others would counter that his decisions have nearly led to the decimation of the world's largest financial system. Who is correct?

If Wall Street had a chisel, Alan Greenspan's smiling face would today be carved on Mount Rushmore. From the late 1980s until just recently, the Maestro, as an admiring journalist styled him, could seemingly do no wrong. He set interest rates[1]—always, so his fans insisted—the right rates. He presided over an economy that only rarely stumbled into recession or crisis. And when it did lose its way, the Greenspan Fed could be counted on to ease the pain with freshly printed dollars and low interest rates.

The archetypical central banker is dour and fretful, but Greenspan broke the mold. Polite, self-effacing, and pleasant, he gave no offense, even when badgered by his critics in the endless congressional hearings to which every Fed Chairman is subjected. He could scold and worry—usually on matters over which the Fed had no control—but his characteristic posture was one of sunny optimism. The computer revolution, financial innovation, and the globalization of trade and investment were, for him, developments of immense promise. Don't worry, he assured the United States. Wall Street heartily agreed. The future glowed bright. Newly printed dollars and low interest rates were a fabulous stimulant for investment assets and real estate.

But consider how your own life has changed over the last few years. How have Greenspan's actions affected your stock portfolio, 401(k), or mortgage? Will you be better off for having lived through the Greenspan era, or will you be much poorer for having done so?

The truth is that the majority of Greenspan's decisions as Fed Chairman from August 11, 1987, to January 31, 2006, were not beneficial to you, nor did they leave the country better off, despite Greenspan's glowing self-critique in his own book, *The Age of Turbulence*. In reality, the overwhelming majority of people in the United States will find that they are worse off in the years ahead as a result of his stewardship.

Some might ask, "He's the Fed *Chairman*; how could he have been wrong?" My response is: Greenspan erred by continually picking an interest rate that was too low, then he solved the turmoil that resulted from that decision with *another* period of interest rates that were *again* too low. The result was that, during his reign, the United States experienced a bubble in stocks and then in real estate.[2] These two massive bubbles emerged within 10 years of each other. Prior to Greenspan's arrival at the Fed, excluding the brief mania for commodities and precious metals from late 1979 to early 1980, *the country had been bubble-free for over 50 years.*

Central bankers like Greenspan aren't *bankers* at all. Anyone who thinks a central bank like the Federal Reserve performs any function remotely similar to those they've experienced in their local branch banks would be wrong. Central bankers are actually central *planners*. Like bureaucratic leaders of central-planned or command economies, they pick an interest rate to within two decimal places that they guess will be the correct one, and then they proceed to cram it down the throat of the banking system.

It is oddly ironic that a small group like the Federal Open Market Committee (FOMC),[3] similar to those found at all levels of any former communist regime, would be in charge of the world's largest and most successful capitalist country—that is, the United States of America and its $13 trillion economy. Given that human beings are not omniscient—and historically central planning committees have been notoriously prone to error—it's easy to imagine that such a group would be far more likely to pick the wrong interest rate than they would be to choose exactly the right one to run an economy. Yet, when these central planners decide they've chosen the wrong rate, for whatever reason, they use the very same process when selecting a new one. It's an impossible job—but they seem happy to do it.

The mission of the Federal Reserve is supposed to be one mainly concerned with stability and prudence. The Fed's own Web site (www.federalreserve.gov) lists its three primary responsibilities to the public as follows:

1. Conducting the nation's monetary policy by influencing money and credit conditions in the economy in pursuit of full employment and *stable* prices;

2. Supervising and regulating banking institutions to ensure the *safety* and *soundness* of the nation's banking and financial system and to protect the credit rights of consumers;

3. Maintaining the *stability* of the financial system and containing systemic risk that may arise in financial markets.

That sounds straightforward enough, even if pursuing stable prices *and* full employment leads to conflicting agendas at certain times. The mission is clear, though the execution of it in real life is far more complex and difficult than it may seem at first. That said, Greenspan's errors in judgment seemed so obvious they beg the questions: Why did he make them? Did he actually set out to redistribute wealth from the middle class to the rich, while the country itself essentially burned the furniture for heat? After all, his bubbles made the sponsors of those bubbles fabulously wealthy, ultimately to the detriment of the average person and the United States as a whole. Or was he simply not up to the task?

With the benefit of hindsight, anyone can look infallible or rewrite his own history, as the Chairman has tried to do. However, just as we have a contemporaneous record of what Greenspan really said, I have a record of my own as well. I began writing an online column about the stock market in mid-1996 and continue to do so to this day. As any longtime reader of those columns can attest, I have certainly not been infallible. Far from it. I saw the stock market[4] bubble building and concluded it would end in disaster—about four years too soon! Then again, I never pretended to know what the right interest rate to run the country was.

In any case, many of those columns were devoted to Greenspan's actions and my objections to them. Others chronicled what transpired in and around the stock market. Consequently, it is possible to judge the Chairman's behavior in real time by looking at various vignettes from those old, wild days via my columns,[5] which we shall do occasionally throughout this book. More importantly, we will review direct quotes from the transcripts[6] of meetings that Greenspan chaired at the FOMC and compare them to what he told the public, the press, and Congress. It is my belief that this book renders a true accounting of Greenspan's almost two-decade tenure at the Fed, and that the evidence speaks for itself.

Down through financial history, markets have intermittently gone to excess. Prices go to the sky and then fall through the floor. Human beings can't help themselves. But the bubbles in U.S. stocks and real estate didn't just happen. To a degree that the American public has not yet fully realized, these costly distortions were instigated and financed by the Federal Reserve—Alan Greenspan's Federal Reserve.

Chapter 1

How Wrong Can One Man Be?

(1973–1994)

An examination of Greenspan's record as an economic forecaster shows that he was less than stellar, from his 1973 statement that "it is very rare that you can be as unqualifiedly bullish as you can be now" just as the worst U.S. recession since the Great Depression was about to unfold, to his support for the deregulation of the S&L industry as a paid consultant for Lincoln Savings and Loan. How could Greenspan miss the risk in the S&L industry that cost taxpayers over $100 billion when it imploded? And that's just the start.

Alan Greenspan wasn't always a central planner. Prior to becoming Fed Chairman, he was president of his own consulting firm, Townsend-Greenspan, from 1954 until 1987. He also served in various government capacities; for example, he was a member of the commission to end the draft and a member of the Social Security Commission. But his most visible position before he became Fed chief was chairman of the president's Council of Economic Advisers (CEA), which he headed from 1974 to early 1977.

Inquiring minds might like to know what sort of a track record he left behind.

An interesting vantage point from which to make that determination would be Greenspan's Senate confirmation hearing. (A prospective Fed Chairman needs Congressional approval.) On July 21, 1987, he appeared before the Senate Committee on Banking, Housing, and Urban Affairs, chaired by Senator William Proxmire of Wisconsin. Proxmire, who had apparently studied all the forecasts made by the CEA from 1976 to 1986, noted that Greenspan's council had "a dismal forecasting record."

Senator Proxmire found that forward-looking projections made during Greenspan's term for 1976 to 1978 were "way off." When it came to forecasting interest rates, the Senator discovered, the man who would become the future interest rate picker for the world's largest economy, made predictions that were wrong *by the largest margin of those made during the period under review.*

Greenspan's errors, in Proxmire's words, *"broke all records for the entire period."*

You could say Greenspan was off by a bit, as his prophecy for the ending rate on Treasury bills in 1978 was 4.4 percent. It turned out to be 9.8 percent. He did no better guessing at the future rate of inflation for that same year—it soared at an annual rate of 9.2 percent, versus his prediction of 4.5 percent.

Greenspan's response to Proxmire? "That is not my recollection of the way the forecasts went."

Proxmire then read the forecasts to the candidate, forcing him to admit, "well, if they're written down, those are the numbers." But Greenspan wasn't finished trying to rewrite history. He attempted to throw Proxmire off, complaining that "there is a very substantial difference, Senator, between forecasting in the Administration and forecasting outside." But the Senator was having none of it. He shot back: "Every one of the chairmen of the CEA had the same problem, and they didn't miss as much as you did—*not nearly as much.*"

As the hearings drew to a close, Proxmire said, [hopefully] "when you get to the Federal Reserve Board, everything will come up roses. *You can't always be wrong.*" To which the man who would come to be called the

"Maestro" responded, "All I can suggest to you, Senator, is that the rest of my career has been somewhat more successful." Really?

Greenspan at this point was either in denial or attempting to revise his own history. Let's review some examples from Greenspan's track record before his appointment as top man at the Fed.

On January 7, 1973, Greenspan made a bold prediction to the *New York Times*: "It is very rare that you can be as unqualifiedly bullish as you can be now." He was spectacularly wrong. Four days later the Dow Jones Industrial Average peaked at 1051 and then declined by 46 percent over the next two years as the country endured the worst recession since the Great Depression.

As monumental a mistake as that was, it wasn't Greenspan's only error during that period of time. On September 5, 1974, the day after he was sworn in as CEA chairman, he proclaimed, "We are not about to get a dramatic decrease in economic activity." Yet, that is *precisely* what transpired as the economy shrank by 5.8 percent from mid-1974 to mid-1975. Was the Maestro finally on point when he began to worry in April 1975 when he pronounced to a New York audience that the worst was yet to come? Not exactly. The recession had ended a month earlier in March 1975. Suffice it to say, that economic contraction fooled the future Fed Chairman both coming and going.

Another notable example of poor judgment made during his consulting days at Townsend-Greenspan, though one which would not become obvious until after he became Fed Chairman, was his wrongheaded view of the business practices of certain savings and loans (S&Ls) in the mid-1980s. These practices erupted into the S&L crisis, which led to the recession of the early 1990s.

In his book, *Inside Job: The Looting of America's Savings and Loans*, Stephen Pizzo describes an encounter in 1984 between Greenspan and Ed Gray (who was then the Federal Home Loan Bank board chairman) that bears repeating:

> Gray received a letter from respected economist Alan Greenspan telling him he should stop worrying so much. Greenspan wrote that *deregulation* was working just as planned, and he named 17 thrifts that had reported record profits and were prospering under the new rules. Greenspan wrote the letter while he was a paid consultant for Lincoln Savings and Loan of Irvine, CA, owned by a Charles Keating, Jr. Four years after Greenspan wrote the letter to Gray, 15 of the 17 thrifts he'd cited would be out of business and would cost the FSLIC $3 billion in losses.[1]

And then, in a Febuary 13, 1985, letter to Thomas Sharkey, Principal Supervisory Agent for the Federal Home Loan Bank of San Francisco, Greenspan made the specific pronouncement that the management of the Keating thrift enterprise Lincoln Savings and Loan was "seasoned and expert in selecting and making direct investments." In addition, he noted, "management has a long and continuous record of outstanding success in making sound and profitable investments." He concluded that the institution "presents no foreseeable risk to the Federal Savings and Loan Insurance Corporation." Lincoln Savings and Loan was seized by Federal regulators in 1989, and its eventual cleanup cost the taxpayers over $2.5 billion.

The reckless policies pursued by many S&Ls led to the collapse of that entire industry—an event that figured prominently in the recession the country experienced in 1990 and 1991. Greenspan's lack of understanding regarding the out-of-control lending practices of those institutions was one reason he did not recognize that economic contraction as it was unfolding—though he would later claim that not only did he see it coming, but that his swift actions prevented it from becoming worse. In some ways, the S&L crisis was a precursor to the undisciplined, runaway lending that led to the housing crisis of 2007. (We'll discuss this in greater detail in Chapter 7.)

In testimony before the Senate Banking Committee in May 1994, and with the benefit of hindsight, Greenspan delivered his explanation of what the Fed had done and why:

> In the spring of 1989, we began to ease monetary conditions as we observed the consequence of balance-sheet strains resulting from increased debt. Households and businesses became much more reluctant to borrow and spend, and lenders to extend credit—a phenomenon often referred to as the "credit crunch." In an endeavor to defuse these financial strains, we moved short-term rates lower in a long series of steps through the summer of 1992, and we held them at unusually low levels through the end of 1993—both absolutely, and, importantly, relative to inflation.

While that is an accurate assessment of what the Fed had done, it is completely misleading in its inference that the Fed's actions were due to foresight on the part of Greenspan and company, as is made clear by examining Greenspan's previous testimony from four years earlier.

In January 1990, Greenspan testified before the Joint Economic Committee, just prior to the failure of Drexel Burnham Lambert, the firm that Mike Milken turned into the infamous junk bond powerhouse. Drexel's demise was a significant milestone in the leveraged credit problems of 1989 through 1992. In his statements, the Chairman didn't dwell on junk bonds, junk loans, failing banks, or generically on "the consequence of balance-sheet strains resulting from increased debt," as he would put it in the May 1994 Senate appearance. Although Greenspan did mention commercial real estate, he did not suggest that interest rates would be progressively lowered to reduce the financial strains that would become so obvious to him four years later. "But such imbalances and dislocations as we see in the economy today probably do not suggest anything more than a temporary hesitation in the continuing expansion of the economy," he recapped in that 1990 appearance. He reiterated his optimistic viewpoint during an August 1990 — the first official month of the budding recession — FOMC meeting: "Those who argue that we are already in recession I think are reasonably certain to be wrong...."

At a news conference on July 10, 1991, Greenspan rendered this upbeat assessment of the economy, which had touched its official low point in March 1991 (it should be noted that the official start and end dates for a recession are determined by the National Bureau of Economic Research, but not until well after the fact): "I think the evidence is increasing week by week that the bottom is passed and the economy is beginning to move up.... I think it's a pretty safe bet at this stage to conclude that the decline is behind us and the outlook is continuing to improve."

Eureka! Greenspan had actually been exactly right — the economy had bottomed and was turning up. However, by October of that year his perspective had changed and he began to use the phrase "economic headwinds," a term he would use often to describe the debt predicament that he only *then* saw holding back the economy. From May 1989, when the rate cutting began, until July 1991, a period of time when Greenspan was remarkably cheerful about an economy that was weakening, he cut rates by about 36 percent, from 9 percent to 5.75 percent.

However, from summer 1991—roughly six months after the economy had bottomed—until the time Greenspan was finally finished lowering interest rates in September 1992, he had slashed them by another 44 percent to 3 percent, where he held them for an additional 15 months.

It wasn't until February 4, 1994, that rates were *raised for the first time in five years.*

To review: Greenspan cut rates enough while he was still sanguine about the economy to get it growing again. Yet, because he didn't recognize the recovery—just as he missed the economic contraction—he cut rates too much and held them too low for too long, thereby massively *overstimulating* the financial markets. (This is a sin he's guilty of committing time and again.) In doing so, he succeeded in driving baby boomers (and members of the American Association of Retired Persons, AARP) out of certificates of deposit (CDs) and bonds into stocks in a desperate attempt on their part to replace the yields that had disappeared.

Greenspan's actions on the interest rate front corroborate a critical assessment of his understanding of the economic environment during the period from 1989 through early 1994. Let's dig a little deeper.

The year 1994 offers up many clues about Alan Greenspan, the man, as it presents us with plenty of nuggets of information with which to assess his perspective on his own viewpoint. If we contrast what he said publicly and privately (via subsequently released transcripts that are made available by the FOMC after a five-year lag) that year, with his more recent version of that period presented in various interviews surrounding his book tour, some rather striking inconsistencies emerge. First, let's look at the economic landscape as he described it in his own words in testimony before the Senate on May 27, 1994:

> Since the latter part of 1993, however the expansionary effects of the monetary policy of the past few years have become increasingly apparent. . . . GDP clearly has accelerated. Strength has been particularly evident in interest-sensitive sectors. Business investment has been quite robust, and order books for producers of durable equipment have expanded appreciably. Housing starts rose in the last three months of 1993 to their highest level in over four

years; although they have dropped back some more recently, they remain 18 percent above a year ago. Demand for motor vehicles has been strong, lifting production of many types of automobiles and light trucks to capacity.

Moreover, as economic conditions have improved in other industrial countries, the growth in our merchandise exports has picked up markedly. Overall industrial capacity utilization has increased to 83½ percent, its highest level since the late 1980s. In excess of two million jobs have been created over the past twelve months, and the unemployment rate has fallen substantially…. Given the stronger economic and financial conditions, it became evident by early 1994 that the mission of monetary policy of the last few years had been accomplished. The "headwinds" were substantially reduced, and the expansion appeared solid and self-sustaining.

Having finally declared victory over the economic slump that snuck up on him in late 1989, Greenspan was ready to discuss his thought process concerning interest rate hikes:

Having met our objective, we confronted the question of whether there was any reasonable purpose in maintaining the stimulative level of interest rates held throughout 1993. The answer to that question was no.... The question that remained was how to implement this shift. The economy looked quite robust, but we were concerned about the *effects on financial markets of a rapid move away from accommodation.* [italics mine] Short-term rates had remained unusually low for a long time, and long-term rates persisted well above the short-term rates. The resulting attractiveness of holding stocks and bonds was further enhanced by a nearly unbroken stream of capital gains as long-term rates fell, which imparted the false impression that returns on long-term investments were not only quite high, but consistently so.

During this testimony, Greenspan even described the effect that driving rates to 3 percent had on the public:

[L]ured by consistently high returns in capital markets, people exhibited increasing willingness to take on market risk by extending the maturity of their investments. In retrospect, it is evident that all sorts of investors made this change in strategy—from the very sophisticated to the much less experienced. One especially notable feature of the shift was the large and accelerating pace of flows into stock and bond mutual funds in recent years. In 1993 alone, $281 billion moved into these funds, representing the *lion's* share [italics mine] of net investment in the U.S. bond and stock markets. A significant portion of the investments in longer-term mutual funds undoubtedly was diverted from deposits, money market funds, and other short-term lower yielding, but less speculative instruments.

This phenomenon tied Greenspan's hands to some degree, because now that he had herded all the little fish into the stock market pool, he appeared to be leery of suffocating them if he drained out liquidity too rapidly, as his testimony continued:

Because we at the Federal Reserve were concerned about sharp reactions in markets that had *grown accustomed to an unsustainable combination of high returns and low volatility,* we chose a cautious approach to our policy actions, moving by small amounts at first. Members of the Federal Open Market Committee agreed that excess monetary accommodation had to be eliminated expeditiously, and a rapid shift would not in itself have been expected to destabilize the economy. We recognized, however, that our shift could impart uncertainty to markets, and many of us were concerned that a large immediate move in rates *would create too big a dose of uncertainty* which could destabilize the financial system, indirectly affecting the real economy…. Thus, we judged at our

May 17 meeting that we could initiate a larger adjustment, without undue adverse market reaction. [italics mine]

Here, we see the very earliest public hint that Greenspan was not prepared to take action that could potentially hurt the stock market—the first evidence of what would come to be known as the *Greenspan Put*.[2] He was obviously quite pleased with himself, adding that "indeed, markets reacted quite positively, on balance."

Voilá! He had threaded the needle. The tightening process was underway, and the damage proved to be manageable as the stock market had shrugged off the most recent one-half percentage point hike in rates.

That congressional soliloquy, however, doesn't quite jibe with what Greenspan had told members of the FOMC behind closed doors just 10 days previously:

[T]he mere fact that uncertainty did not exist was not good; it clearly was bad. And our endeavor [was] to break that pattern.… As a consequence we have taken a very significant amount of air out of the bubble.… I think there's still a lot of bubble around; we have not completely eliminated it. Nonetheless, we have the capability, I would say at this stage, to move more strongly than we usually do without the risk of cracking the system.

These comments are in line with ones he had made the month before, at the April 18 FOMC meeting, where he stated:

> The sharp declines in stock and bond prices since our last meeting, I think, have defused a significant part of the bubble which had previously built up. We let a lot of air out of the tire, so to speak.

Bubble? How interesting. In the future, the Chairman would repeatedly state (until approximately 2004) that bubbles were extremely difficult if not impossible to identify. For example, in a noteworthy speech in August 2002, Greenspan pleaded that "it was very difficult to definitively identify a bubble until after the fact—that is, when its bursting confirmed its existence." I'm sure it's a great comfort to folks to know that after a bubble collapses and they have lost money, the Fed will be able to recognize that there *had* been a bubble. However, this quote appears to be just an attempt to avoid blame for the post-2000 stock market implosion, as Greenspan seems pretty certain of his ability to spot and deal with a bubble in 1994. After all, here he was discussing what he might do and what he had done thus far about the bubble he felt had developed.

Readers might wonder who the *real* Alan Greenspan was: the man before the Senate, the man addressing the FOMC, or the man giving the speech in 2002. Here's another good question: if Greenspan really felt a bubble was underway, why didn't he publicly say something about the dangers a bubble creates? Or, for starters, why not raise margin requirements?[3] For that matter, why not raise rates even more aggressively, since the Fed, to paraphrase the Chairman, had the capability to move more strongly than usual? Why even be concerned about the possibility of an "undue adverse market reaction" if you were really worried a bubble was forming? Why not deal with the issue before it became too serious? Any moderately thorough reading of history shows that it is far better to prevent a bubble from building than to try and deal with the aftermath.

Greenspan apparently had little interest in nipping problems in the bud, preferring instead to clean up whatever mess he left behind with the same actions that started the problem—namely, *easy money*. At a lunch sponsored by the BMO Financial Group on October 6, 2006, Greenspan was asked a lengthy but important question by Dr. Sherry Cooper:

What do you tell people who accuse your Fed of creating the stock market bubble of the late 1990s? Despite your disparagement of "irrational exuberance" with respect to tech stocks in December 1996, you aggressively increased the provision of credit in 1999 in response to Y2K fears. Many have argued that this fuelled [*sic*] the 86 percent rise in the Nasdaq that year which, of course, ended very badly in March of 2000. Don't you think this easy-money policy contributed to the wild IPOs and the over-investment, further inflating the tech bubble? Why did you not respond with at least an increase in margin requirements or a tighter provision of credit?

We will deal with other aspects of that question in Chapters 3 and 4, but his answer was surprising; it focused on the particular period we have been reviewing:

We tried that in 1994/95 and failed. We learned that the Fed could not incrementally diffuse [*sic*] a bubble. We tried in 1994 when we raised interest rates—you remember—even by 75 basis points. It was highly disruptive.… And in the end, we failed. The stock market bubble had already been forming, and didn't react to the tightening. We didn't diffuse [*sic*] the bubble; we made it worse. The stock market was flat during the tightening period, and when the tightening ended in 1995, the stock market took off. We realized that unless we tightened aggressively enough to hurt the economy and profitability, the market bubble wouldn't diffuse [*sic*]. Rates would have had to go up 10-to-12 percentage points (1,000 to 1,200 basis points) to break the back of the stock market, which would destroy the economy. Therefore, we realized we couldn't diffuse the bubble, and decided to focus instead [*sic*] on dealing with the aftermath, not the bubble itself. We didn't ease until 2001 because we wanted to be certain that the bubble was over.

This lengthy answer is filled with inaccuracies. It's worth dwelling on for a moment because it so clearly illuminates the optimistic interpretation of the Chairman's 2006 view of his prior decade's work. For starters, at the FOMC meeting on August 16, 1994, Greenspan declared: "With the May move [Author's note: which was the hike that occurred at the previous meeting, which we just reviewed], I think we clearly demonstrated that the bubble for all practical purposes had been defused...."

Greenspan savored his victory at the FOMC meeting on February 1, 1995, when the Fed would raise interest rates for the last time until March 1997:

One can say that while the stock market is not low, it clearly is not anywhere close to being as elevated as it was a year or so ago in relative terms. [Author's note: It's not clear exactly what he means here, as the actual price for the S&P 500 Index was flat to slightly higher than it was the year before.] We have taken a lot of bubble out of the market. Indeed, I would think one of the successes of our policy to date is that we have taken the degrees of instability that one can envisage in stock prices down to a much reduced level of concern.

Let's return to his previously noted protestations from 2006. Greenspan is correct that the Fed failed. But it failed because it *declared victory* when it had achieved no such thing. They not only stopped raising interest rates in February 1995, but were back cutting them again by July. Thus, Greenspan is exactly correct when he states, "we didn't diffuse [*sic*] the bubble; we made it worse." Anyone who looks at a long-term chart of the stock market averages will see that the slope of the line changes quite dramatically in 1995. The reason is, as the man said, the Fed made it *worse*. (And they would make it even more worse before they were through. See Figure 1.)

Greenspan's claims that the tightening was highly disruptive is not evident in the action of the stock market through that period, though some leveraged players in fixed income did get wiped out. But that is what is supposed to happen to those in free markets who take too much risk. Creative destruction is part of capitalism. As for the wild conjecture that interest rates would need to rise to 10 to 12 percent to break the back of the stock market, we will never know because interest rates were never even north of 6 percent in 1994–1995, after hav-

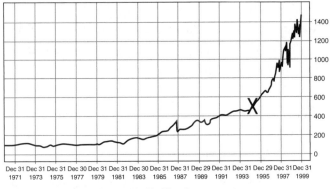

Dec 31 Dec 31 Dec 31 Dec 30 Dec 31 Dec 31 Dec 30 Dec 31 Dec 31 Dec 29 Dec 31 Dec 31 Dec 29 Dec 31 Dec 31
1971 1973 1975 1977 1979 1981 1983 1985 1987 1989 1991 1993 1995 1997 1999

Figure was created with data provided by Bloomberg

Figure 1 Did Something Happen in 1995?

ing been 7 percent at the end of 1990 and 9 percent in 1989. As for the claim "we didn't ease until 2001 because we wanted to be certain that the bubble was over," it isn't quite clear from this quote, but Greenspan appears to shift his answer from addressing his actions in the 1994–1995 period to what he did in 2001, which we will cover in Chapters 5 and 6.

However, Greenspan didn't ease until 2001, not because "we wanted to be certain that the bubble was over," but because he wasn't aware there had been an actual bubble at that time. As Greenspan's optimism from 2000 will show, he thought all was well (just as he did in 1990) and only started cutting rates when he belatedly realized that the economy was falling apart.

Chapter 2

The Bubble King: The Put Is Born
(1995–1997)

The year 1995 marks the start of the biggest stock market bubble this country has ever experienced. Baby boomers, captivated by the Internet and the new financial networks like CNBC, believe they possess the know-how to invest for themselves and had earned the right to be rich. In addition to being the cheerleader for the miracle of productivity, Greenspan throws gasoline on a fire in the form of continual interest rate cuts, and fuels a mania.

July 1995 marked the start of the biggest stock market bubble the United States has ever experienced. A rational person might ask what on earth caused Greenspan to shift from self-proclaimed bubble fighter to bubble blower in such a short period of time. One answer might be: his *imagination*.

The rate cutting began without much provocation. Nowhere in the five pages of text from the July 1995 meeting's transcript, where the Chairman lays out his case for a rate cut from 6 percent to 5.75 percent, does he offer any solid evidence that one is needed. Greenspan admitted as much in the penultimate paragraph: "I have concluded that, since the risks are beginning to ease slightly, there is no urgency here; but I do think we should move because I find it increasingly difficult to argue in favor of staying where we are unless one can argue that inflationary pressures are still building."

What about the bubble that Greenspan had just paid so much lip service to and would later claim to have battled against so diligently? He never mentioned the word *bubble*. One might have expected that had Greenspan been serious about defusing it, that alone would have provided him with ammunition to be able to argue in favor of staying put. In the discussion that followed his call to lower rates, not even the single dissenting voter—Federal Reserve District president Thomas Hoenig—mentioned the word. It was as if none of them had ever heard of or were concerned about the bubble. Immediately following the vote, someone asked if there would be a press release. Greenspan responded, attributing his comment solely to himself and not to the Federal Reserve Board: "I am sorry. The draft reads as follows, 'Chairman Alan Greenspan announced today that the Federal Open Market Committee (FOMC) decided to decrease slightly the degree of pressure on reserve positions. As a result of the monetary tightening initiated in early 1994, inflationary pressures have receded enough to accommodate a modest adjustment in monetary conditions.'" It was clear that Greenspan had prepared the text ahead of time, and he admitted as much later in the meeting. He had decided to cut rates and apparently no one was going to stop him. No one, however, tried to.

At this point in the year the stock market was roughly 20 percent higher than it was at the start of the prior year, and about 20 percent higher than when Greenspan was musing about a bubble. Inexplicably, by the end of 1995 there was no new talk of a bubble by Greenspan, even though the market was nearly 35 percent higher than when the word was first bandied about. But the party was only just getting started.

Bubbles are rare. They have occurred occasionally throughout history—even in the absence of a central bank sponsor. Consider the Dutch tulip craze. In the early seventeenth century, the Netherlands enjoyed an economic revival bolstered by the burgeoning textile trade. Construction and housing prices were at an all-time high. The most exclusive status symbol of wealth was the tulip bulb, professionally grown and possessed only by the upper class. Ownership of multiple high-end bulbs was a symbol of power and prestige.

As bulb growing proliferated, the middle class realized just how much the wealthy spent on tulip bulbs—and how much they made buying and selling them. At that time, the average yearly income in Amsterdam was about 150 florins, but a single coveted bulb easily sold for over six times that amount. Taverns became stock markets for trading, and the public piled in. Unregulated tulip futures were created to satisfy demand. Farmers, bakers, and shoemakers all saw an easy way to make money with no risk, and they sold businesses, farms, and homes to trade tulip bulbs. At the top of that bubble, prices rose twentyfold in a single month. Out of nowhere, in February 1637, the tulip market suddenly crashed and the price of some of the most exotic bulbs collapsed in six weeks from the equivalent of $75,000 to $1. Panic ensued, and thousands of Dutch citizens were financially ruined.

As the Tulip Mania illustrates, sometimes when market conditions are just right, the madness of the crowd takes over and bizarre results follow. But when the right economic conditions meet an aggressive central bank

with a proclivity to print money, a truly large and ultimately destructive bubble will result. That was what happened in the United States in the late 1920s, which
culminated in the stock market crash of 1929. The consequences of that bubble led to the Great Depression.

But in the late 1990s, Greenspan took a much more
active role in the process than any Fed member had during the Roaring Twenties. Whether providing fuel for the
fire in the form of easy money, or rationalizations that people could use as their reason to speculate, Greenspan was
the poster boy for the developing bubble. He wasn't the
only reason there was a bubble, but without his sponsor-
ship it could never have grown anywhere near as large or
as dangerous as it did. So, what were the factors that created a financial environment so conducive to speculation?

First on the list: demographics. The baby boomers'
awareness that investing for retirement was becoming
critically important fostered a *need to believe* in the mind
of the public. Wall Street did its part by supplying the
rationalizations as well as the merchandise to the eager
masses. Second, the impressive technology improvements experienced in the United States and elsewhere
created the objects of speculation and fostered the giddy
mood necessary for baby boomers to want to speculate.

It's easy to understand why technology is such a financial aphrodisiac. Life without big-screen televisions, fax
machines, iPods, or cell phones would be far less enjoy-
able, while life without drugs such as Viagra or Lipitor

would be boring and shorter. Yet nothing heretofore had so seemingly demystified and so dramatically altered the investing landscape the way the personal computer (PC) had. It simultaneously empowered the masses to believe that they were in complete control of their investment choices and deluded them into confusing information with knowledge—a dangerous combination. The role of Microsoft Windows 95 in the process of seducing the crowd cannot be overemphasized. Windows 95 made personal computers far friendlier while making communication between PCs far easier, which in turn spurred the explosion in the number of people utilizing the Internet. More importantly, in addition to being incredibly useful, the Internet helped to supply the imagination component necessary to get folks really excited about how rich they might become, which served to further intensify speculation.

Third, the popularity of business and finance programming such as that at CNBC (or "Bubblevision," as I nicknamed it in 1999) helped seduce the public into an overconfident state of knowledge bordering on arrogance. People became certain that they possessed the know-how to invest for themselves and thus had earned the right to be rich.

Lastly, corporate America itself—the object of all this speculation—enthusiastically elevated accounting into pure art. They didn't fuel speculation through their actual earnings but through the creative expression of those earnings. One-time charges, merger-related write-offs, forward-looking statements about the improvement in business trends, and stock options with their attendant absurd tax treatment were the new tools of the trade. That said, corporate America didn't actually help create the euphoria; instead, the euphoria allowed questionable practices to flourish.

Collectively, the factors just described as well as Greenspan's willingness to continually throw gasoline on a fire in the form of easy money convinced the masses that the only real risk associated with stocks was in not owning them. In short, it was an incredibly fertile period for speculation, and with Alan Greenspan in control of the punch bowl it is easy to see why the public behaved as they did. What is not clear is why *Greenspan* behaved as he did. The reason seems to be that he was infatuated with the concept of productivity.

According to transcripts from the August 1995 FOMC meeting (the meeting that followed the one in which interest rates had been cut to 5.75 percent), a new Greenspan thesis began to emerge:

> There is a major statistical problem. We are all acutely aware that there has been a shift towards an increasingly conceptual and impalpable value

added and that actual GDP in constant dollars is becoming progressively less visible. All of these intellectual services have historically tended to be written off as expenses in income statements, research and development clearly being the largest and most obvious of these. We are moving towards an economy in which the value added is increasingly software, telecommunication technologies, and various means of conveying value to people without the transference of a physical good; entertainment is the obvious classical case. So we are getting increasing evidence that we are probably expensing items that really should be capitalized. [Author's note: That is, they should be treated as an *asset*, not as an *expense*.] This is the issue with software. We have seen, I think you are aware, a number of industries in which the stock market value to book value is much higher than one. In fact, in certain industries it is a huge multiple. The trend of market to book value has been rising dramatically over the years, and I suspect we cannot extract all of that from changing market valuations of stocks in general. What appears to be the case is that an increasing amount of capital expenditures in the classic sense is being misclassified as expenses, and that obviously lowers the book value of the firm to well below where it would be if those expenses had been appropriately capitalized. The stock market is basically telling us that there has indeed been an acceleration of productivity if one properly incorporates in output that which the markets value as output. If in effect there has been a failure to capture all the output that has been occurring, we will indeed show *productivity growth that is too low.* [italics mine] It is hard to imagine that productivity is moving up only around 1 percent under the new weighting basis with profit margins moving the way they are and with the widespread business restructuring that is occurring. I think the difficulty is not in productivity; it is at the Department of Commerce [Author's note: where data is calculated].

In other words, the Chairman had an epiphany: the stock market had been on a rampage because productivity was far higher, profits were far greater, and thus stocks were much cheaper than was generally understood. This new thesis became the prism through which Greenspan viewed everything, and as such he interpreted galloping stock prices as validating his theory rather than as being an indication of a bubble—which, in fact, they actually were.

This wasn't the first time in his career, nor was it the last, that the Chairman would draw the wrong conclusion. What was undeniably a bubble—exacerbated, if not created, by Greenspan—was now seen by Greenspan himself as a *rational response* to a new era in the U.S. economy *powered by technology that drove the growth of productivity*. Of course, if the country was more productive, then that implied that the rate of inflation was perhaps overstated. A whole host of conclusions tumbled from Greenspan's new theory.

At the December 1995 FOMC meeting, Greenspan spent a great deal of time expounding on his new theory:

> I want to raise a broad hypothesis about where the economy is going over the longer term and what the underlying forces are.... You may recall that earlier this year I raised the issue of the extraordinary impact of accelerating technologies.... This is a new phenomenon.... One would certainly assume that we would see this in the productivity data, but it is difficult to find it there. In my judgment there are several reasons, the most important of which is that the data are lousy.... Looking at market values, we are not capitalizing various types of activities properly. In the past, we looked at capital expenditures only as spending on a blast furnace or a steel rolling mill. Now improvement in the value of a firm is influenced by such factors as how much in-house training they have and what type. That creates economic value in the stock market sense, and we are not measuring it properly.

The Chairman also spent time explaining that these changes also seemed to be holding down the inflation rate, noting that "finally, it is very difficult to find typical inflationary forces anywhere in the world.... But I would suspect that if we did not have these technological changes going on, our job and that of our counterparts abroad would have been materially more difficult."

Greenspan came to the conclusion that there was no bubble underway because technology expenditures weren't accounted for correctly, meaning that stock prices weren't nearly as high as they seemed. And even more importantly, technology was working its magic via productivity gains, which meant that the inflation rate was also overstated. As much as the Chairman would wax poetic over technology and productivity in the coming years, it was keeping the inflation rate in check that allowed him to keep the money spigots open wide for most of his reign.

In fact, a large financial asset bubble can occur only at moments in history when inflation is low. If inflation is high, a central bank is expected to combat it with tighter money and higher interest rates. An absolutely essential component of the late-1990s' stock bubble was a well-behaved rate of inflation. Of course the rate of inflation is a function of what is measured and how it is measured. All throughout the 1995–1997 period, Greenspan threw his weight behind a move afoot to prove that the inflation rate was overstated—a movement *he* had started.

Testifying before the Senate and House Budget Committee on January 10, 1995, Greenspan told the committee that the inflation rate was probably overstated by 0.5 percent to 1.5 percent. If the overstatement were true, it would be a windfall for the government. Expenditures indexed to inflation, like social security, could be cut and the public would never know. Politicians could put the money to other uses. He suggested that the anomaly be investigated. It was.

"The Advisory Commission to Study the Consumer Price Index (aka The Boskin Commission) was appointed by the Senate Finance Committee to study the role of the CPI in government benefit programs and to make recommendations for any needed changes in the CPI." So stated the synopsis of the commission mandate that preceded its interim report, published on September 15, 1995. It found that the inflation rate was overstated by 1.1 percentage points. (In other words, if inflation had previously been estimated at 3 percent, it really had only been 1.9 percent.) Several recommendations were made by the commission to the budget committee and were instituted with great efficiency by the Bureau of Labor Statistics (BLS).

There was no pretense on the Boskin Commission's part that its goal was anything other than to reduce the annual consumer price index (CPI). The report was sub-titled "Toward a More Accurate Measure of the Cost of Living." The objective was not to improve—or even address—the accuracy of the change in prices. Its main purpose was to measure the influence of the CPI on the cost of government programs. The bottom line? It was not an impartial study of how government price calcula-tions affected programs; instead, it was intended to reduce government costs. Greg Mankiw, Chairman of George W. Bush's Council of Economic Advisers from 2003 to 2005, said at the time that "the debate about the CPI was really a political debate about how, and by how much, to cut real entitlements." It appears they had an agenda: to reduce the government's estimate of the rate of inflation.

And reduce it they did—by far more than 1.1 percent. (Though no sane shopper would ever agree with their methodologies, many would get caught up in the low inflation hype when it came to stock market speculation.)

Three important changes that dramatically warped the inflation data were implemented. The first and most straightforward was to switch the period-to-period CPI calculations from arithmetic to geometric. This change sounds innocent enough, but let's look at its impact. Say that the price of a hog rises from $100 to $161 over five years. The "annualized" rise, the geometric calculation, is 10 percent a year. The change each year, the arith-metic calculation, is a little over 12 percent (61 divided by 5). Presto, the inflation rate shrinks.

The second change, made to account for substitution effects, was truly absurd. It works like this: let's say the price of beef rises relative to the price of chicken. The Boskin Commission says you will substitute chicken for the beef you previously ate. Thus the rise in the price of chicken will be used in CPI calculations. The fact that you may *not* wish or choose to eat chicken instead of beef is not a consideration.

However, the third change, known as "hedonic adjustments," not only wildly distorted the CPI data, it also allowed for plenty of mischief across the board. The Boskin Commission advised that if a product went up in price but improved in quality, then the increase in price needed to be reduced by the amount of dollars that captured how much the object had been improved. Formerly, when calculating the change in price, the price increase would be a known fact; in the latter type of calculation, the price increase would be less certain, as improvement in quality would obviously be subjective.

Here's an example of the power of hedonic adjustments. The Leuthold Group, a Minneapolis investment research firm, calculated that between 1979 and 2004, the average price paid for a new car in the United States increased from $6,847 to $27,940, a 308 percent increase. Meanwhile, the BLS calculation for the consumer price index only comes to a 71 percent increase for autos over that same period. So, 237 percent of the price increase had been eliminated due to the estimated quality improvement of cars. (The BLS considers airbags to be a quality improvement, which reduces the cost of a car in its calculations, even though the cars cost more because of the airbags.)

Such quality adjustments are used to reduce the price increases for a range of products, including apparel, airfares, gasoline, hospital services, home computers, television sets, microwave ovens, washing machines, clothes dryers, and textbooks. There has never been an adjustment in the opposite direction, for deterioration of quality, which would reveal itself in a higher price than that which is paid by the consumer. Discount air fares do save money, but no adjustment is made for cramped seats or endless delays: what is the cost of lousy service in a service economy?

But the distortions caused by hedonics don't stop there. When the price of a product actually declines and the quality appears to have increased, especially if both change dramatically, the hedonically adjusted price will collapse. Such was the case with the cost of computing power in the late 1990s. As we will see in Chapter 5, given that so many computers were being purchased at that time, the sum total was large enough to distort the productivity and other data for the entire country. For instance, for the year 1998, although only $95.1 billion was actually spent on business computers, the BLS concluded that after hedonic adjustment it was as though business had spent $351.8 billion, which by itself increased real GDP by over 2 percent. In short, the statistical techniques championed by the Boskin Commission are a cheat. The only question is whether they touch U.S. citizens directly or indirectly. Anyone receiving social security payments, a cost-of-living adjustment, or holding an inflation-indexed bond has been impacted directly, as the government has literally taken money out of that person's pocket. Everyone else has been affected indirectly by the distortions created in the economic data, which led to or reinforced many erroneous decisions made by Greenspan and others.

Greenspan delivered his notorious "Irrational Exuberance"[1] speech on December 5, 1996, but nothing he said before or after indicates that he actually took his own message to heart. In fact, at an FOMC meeting 12 days later, while there was plenty of talk about inflation, there was almost no talk of bubbles. What little there was came from FOMC member Lawrence Lindsey, who warned that "1997 [would be] a very good year for irrational exuberance"; he suggested it would create problems that the Fed would have to solve down the road. To which, according to the transcripts, Greenspan glibly responded, "I will make another speech." (Lindsey didn't stick around long after that. He resigned on February 5, 1997.)

The FOMC transcript reveals that Greenspan's pithy comment elicited laughter from the committee. As 1996 drew to a close, with rates holding at 5.25 percent, it had been almost two years since the Fed had stopped tightening (though it had eased three times) and the stock market was now 60 percent higher than when the Chairman began to briefly use the word *bubble*. Greenspan obviously did not believe there was a bubble, apparently he was too busy championing productivity and the new economy to spend much time worrying about one. But 10 years later, after it was clear that a stock market bubble had existed in the mid-to-late 1990s, Greenspan would change his position.

On September 6, 2007, shortly before his autobiography, *The Age of Turbulence*, was to be published, Greenspan gave a speech in Washington, D.C. The *Wall Street Journal* reported that the Chairman claimed that bubbles couldn't be stopped via incremental tightening; that he had tried in 1994–1995, but when he stopped tightening, "prices took off." Greenspan also stated that "we tried to do it again in 1997" and "the same phenomenon occurred."

As we will see in the next chapters, Greenspan didn't try very hard—in fact he barely tried at all. The consequences were even wilder than when he stopped tightening in 1995, but it really didn't seem to matter to him. He believed in a new era. Between the new era and his skills there was nothing for him to fear. In fact, his remarks at the FOMC meeting on March 25, 1997 were more a sermon about how wonderful the economy was than any sort of serious discussion concerning what to do about the bubble that wouldn't die:

> The proposition that inflation has stopped falling is not readily provable. That may seem to be a rather ridiculous statement, but if we look at the data, what we see is that the rate of inflation, no matter how we look at it, has been edging lower with some bumps here and there. [Author's note: No worries on the inflation front; it's still declining.]… The reason is very clearly that productivity is badly underestimated and indeed may actually be accelerating…. [W]e may finally be getting the productivity gains that many have anticipated from the synergies created by the rapidly developing computer technology information structure.
>
> The reason why manufacturers in particular and business people more generally have the view that inflation is dead and the economy is in a new era is that that is the way it feels to them…. Having said all of that, we are not at this stage moving into what I would describe as an overheated boom. We are short of that.
>
> Nonetheless, if we are talking about long-term equilibrium, high market values are better than low market values. What we are trying to avoid is bubbles that break [Author's note: then why not avoid creating them in the first place?], volatility, and the

like, but we are not opposed to the implications of low inflation, which include relatively low risk premiums and fairly strong economic activity. [Author's note: In other words, wild markets are perfectly fine as long as they don't "break" and become "volatile."] I conclude that what we clearly need at this stage is finally to move off the dime. I think that 25 basis points is enough for now [because] … at this stage, the market is expecting 25 basis points. It has discounted such a move, frankly, but it has done so in a positive way, not a negative way. The stock markets are up this morning; the bond market is up. I think that if we were to move 50 basis points today after a long period of doing nothing, though being vigilant if you like, we suddenly would shock the market into thinking that we must feel that we are behind the curve. We are not behind the curve.

In fact, Greenspan was *miles behind the curve.* Nonetheless, though the interest rate hike at this meeting to 5.5 percent was the first one in over two years, it was to be the last one for 15 months (and it would be followed by three rate cuts). In the nine pages of his prepared remarks that day, the only time Greenspan mentions the word *bubble* is in the excerpt above. Like I said, he didn't try very hard, and he certainly made no case whatsoever that day or at the prior meeting for a preemptive move *to rein in the bull,* nor did he even utter the words as he would later claim to have done in his autobiography.

The Standard & Poor's (S&P) 500 gained about 31 percent in 1997, putting the cumulative gain from the early days of bubble talk in 1994 to almost 110 percent. But the mania was still in its early days. The truly extraordinary gains and delusional behavior were still to come.

Chapter 3

The FOMC Meets the Greenspan Put—and Yawns
(1998–1999)

The combination of the collapse of the Russian ruble and the implosion of Long Term Capital Management in 1998 causes the stock market to decline. Greenspan lowers interest rates in September to 5.25 percent...and in a surprising inter-meeting maneuver cuts them again 16 days later despite a healthy market, kicking off a wave of speculation larger than any the United States has ever seen.

In his book *The Age of Turbulence*, Greenspan absolves himself of the blame he deserves for acting so irresponsibly during the later—and truly maniacal—years of the stock market bubble. In the book, Greenspan explains:

> In effect, investors were teaching the Fed a lesson. Bob Rubin [then Secretary of the Treasury] was right. You can't tell when a market is overvalued, and you can't fight market forces. As the boom went on—for three more years, it turned out, greatly increasing the nation's paper wealth—we continually wrestled with the big question of productivity and price stability and other aspects of what people had come to call the New Economy. We looked for other ways to deal with the risk of a bubble. But we did not raise rates any further and we never tried to rein in stock prices again.[1]

It's worth dissecting Greenspan's various points.

First, to say investors were teaching the Fed a lesson is almost humorous. They were just reacting to the policies the Fed was pursuing—an eager willingness to lower interest rates and an extreme reluctance to raise them.

Second, Bob Rubin had nothing to do with the monetary policy. Invoking his name and attempting to have Rubin share in the blame is gratuitous.

Third, the late 1990s didn't witness simply an over-valued market; *the United States experienced the biggest stock market bubble the country had ever experienced*, one that was so out of control you would think that any individual schooled in the fields of finance and economics would be sure to recognize the situation for what it was.

Fourth, you can't fight market forces? As we will see, Greenspan did so *constantly*. He continually tried to fight the forces of creative destruction. Throughout history, markets have risen and fallen, but he tried to thwart the functional equivalent of financial gravity. More importantly, as Fed Chairman, it was incumbent on him to *fight market forces* when they threatened to cause serious long-term damage to the economy. Remember that former Fed Chairman Paul Volcker allowed interest rates to climb to 20 percent briefly in order to break the back of double-digit inflation in the early 1980s. The well-respected former Fed Chairman William McChesney Martin, who chaired the Fed throughout the 1950s and 1960s, stated that the Fed was in "the position of the chaperone who has ordered the punch bowl removed just when the party was really warming up."[2] Greenspan preferred to spike it. Whether through cutting interest rates or giving speeches extolling the virtues of technology and productivity, he was no innocent bystander. Even if he didn't know it, Greenspan contributed to the bubble at every opportunity.

Fifth, as for wrestling with productivity and price stability, mostly he just made speeches affirming how terrific the former was at producing the latter. As for looking for other ways to deal with the risk of a bubble, there is no data to support this claim. He didn't. When the bubble was actually inflating, he didn't see it. Had he seen it and actually been determined to put a halt to the bubble, he would have aggressively raised interest rates, margin requirements, or both. In addition, he could have jawboned about the dangers a bubble presents or used some of the other tools the Fed has at its disposal.

And finally, his last sentence is perhaps the most infuriating. When he says "we never tried to rein in stock prices again," Greenspan makes it sound as if he is telling a fairy tale in which he sat by idly while stocks innocuously drifted higher, everyone became wealthy, and we all lived happily ever after. Nothing could be further from the truth. As we all know, the equity bubble collapsed and Greenspan drove interest rates down to 1 percent in the wake of that collapse. That gave rise to the real estate bubble, which was unwinding in the United States as this book was being written.

In 1998, the stock market had gained about 21 percent for the year through July 20, when it peaked out. The proximate cause for the ensuing decline was the collapse of both the Russian ruble and Long Term Capital Management (that now notorious, highly leveraged hedge fund that imploded in September of that year, which is the subject of the book *When Genius Failed* by Roger Lowenstein). In response to the turmoil caused by these two events, the Fed cut interest rates one-quarter of 1 point at its September 29 FOMC meeting to 5.25 percent.

You can see from Figure 2 (on page 52) that when the Fed acted, the market was not in dire straits; it actually was up a couple of percentage points from where it started the year, while at its *worst* it had only been down a couple of percentage points for the year. In other words no damage had been done. Sure, the year's gains were gone, but that was hardly a crisis—especially when you consider that at the July highs the market was 160 percent higher than it was at the end of 1994, the year of all the Fed bubble talk. Nonetheless, there were strains in the financial system, and this particular rate cut was not all that objectionable. Initially, the market did not respond positively to this rate cut, as it briefly declined a bit. But two weeks later, it rebounded again, and by October 14 it had gained 3.5 percent for the year. That progress, however, apparently was not good enough for Greenspan; the next day he conducted a special intermeeting conference call to discuss the prospects for a surprise rate cut.

Which, in my view, will ultimately come to be seen as *one of the most irresponsible acts in the history of the Federal Reserve.*

Molly Evans

Figure 2 Is There a Reason to Panic?: The Gains for the Year Were Gone, But No Real Damage Had Been Done

A reading of the transcript of the October 15 FOMC meeting reveals that there was no urgent need for such action. About one-third of the way through the meeting, as FOMC members took turns articulating their viewpoints, Cathy Minehan from the Boston Fed—home to some of the world's largest mutual funds—noted: "But, this morning I got a couple calls that suggested, with the Shaw[3] situation having been more or less taken care of the way it was, concerns were easing and that markets seem to have been a lot quieter and more stable over the last couple days, at least to people *directly* in the markets. Have you seen that?"

She was asking the question of Bill McDonough, the head of the New York Fed. He responded, "I have not seen that," adding that his people hadn't either. It seemed that although Boston may have been doing a bit better than it had been, New York appeared not to be in the same enviable position. Philadelphia's Ed Boehne observed, "My sense is business sentiment is eroding. I do not see dramatic erosion at this point, but I think it is clear erosion." On the other hand, Gary Stern from Minneapolis pointed out, "I was struck if anything by what I took to be less concern among our contacts about their own business prospects than I might have expected."

And so it went, with some members more concerned than others, but no one presenting a powerful case to cut interest rates just 16 days after the last rate cut. That said, some rather feeble cases were presented, such as the one offered by Fed governor Alice Rivlin: "Now, we can wait until our next meeting, but that would involve a long wait. The risk of waiting in my view is that we may be forced into a reactive position. The beauty of doing something right now is that *nothing much is happening*." [italics mine]

So even though not much was happening, Rivlin couldn't wait 30 days to cut again. Why? Because she might be in a reactive position? It made no sense, particularly when waiting also meant that she would have some additional data with which to make a better decision. Keep in mind, this was a $10 trillion economy they were talking about; it couldn't shift gears all that fast. Fed governor Ned Gramlich made that point (though he too was arguing to cut rates): "From the standpoint of the real economy, it probably doesn't matter too much; four weeks is not that long a period when we consider all the lags in the real economy. But for the *financial markets*, four weeks could be a long time…." [italics mine]

Aha! The real reason behind the rate cut was the financial markets. There was no real need, as Bill Poole from St. Louis pointed out, to act at that particular moment: "Personally, I would feel a lot better about moving between meetings, given past practice, if there were a sense of urgency that was a step up from a sense of concern." He also cautioned that cutting rates could be seen as "an effort to help bail out the hedge funds."

The outcome of that rate cut turned out to be far worse, as the committee's actions came to be viewed as the Greenspan Put, meaning speculators could take enormous amounts of risk trusting that Greenspan would do anything to stop the market from a serious decline.

The Chairman himself couldn't even make a legitimate case for cutting rates, stating: "The judgments that I am hearing from most of you that nothing much has changed in the economy strikes me as about right." But just because he didn't have a strong case didn't mean that Greenspan wasn't going to cut rates anyway. And so, just 16 days after having cut rates by one-quarter of 1 point, he did it again, taking interest rates down to 5 percent.

In the talk-is-cheap department, Greenspan did make one idle threat, clearly demonstrating that he was willing to cut interest rates at the drop of a hat yet extraordinarily reluctant to raise them (a tendency borne out by his track record). He said: "If in what I would at this point consider to be a relatively low probability the financial markets were to return to what we perceived of as normal two months ago, and if the economy started to strengthen again and the stock market [were] to move higher, there is nothing that would prevent us from reversing our move."

Nothing, that is, except Greenspan himself.

One month later, the market was almost 5 percent higher than where it had been two months prior, but Greenspan not only refused to reverse his move, he also cut rates *again*, this time down to 4.75 percent. (It would take him a full year to reverse the three rate cuts made during the fall of 1998.) However, this particular rate cut was nuclear, kicking off a wave of speculation unlike any ever seen in this country. Since the bubble talk began in early 1994, the Nasdaq and the S&P 500 had performed somewhat similarly. That was about to end. By the time the last rate cut would be rescinded in November 1999, the S&P 500 would gain 35 percent while the Nasdaq would *double* from the day of the surprise rate cut, October 15, 1998. One reason this particular maneuver on the part of the Chairman and company had such a powerful and immediate impact was a function of exactly *when* it happened.

It was the day before an options expiration, that is, when tens of thousands of option contracts expire. All things being equal, expiration Fridays often can be quite volatile, as small price movements around an option strike price can cause large gains or losses since options employ a form of leverage. The time of day added to the violence of the reaction, the news of the surprise rate cut hit the wires with less than an hour left in the trading day. The impact was immediate: *in less than five minutes* the futures market exploded higher by an enormous 5 percent (see Figure 3 on page 57).

It's worth noting that throughout the discussion at the FOMC meeting not one person raised the point that the next day was an option expiration Friday. Whether the committee was unaware of that fact or deemed it unim-

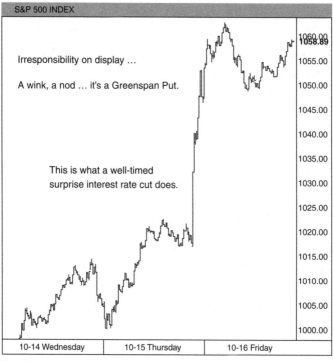

S&P 500 INDEX

Irresponsibility on display …

A wink, a nod … it's a Greenspan Put.

This is what a well-timed
surprise interest rate cut does.

1060.00
1058.89
1055.00
1050.00
1045.00
1040.00
1035.00
1030.00
1025.00
1020.00
1015.00
1010.00
1005.00
1000.00

10-14 Wednesday | 10-15 Thursday | 10-16 Friday

Molly Evans

Figure 3 Anatomy of the Greenspan Put

portant we will never know. But, whatever the reason, it was completely irresponsible of the Fed to spring a totally unnecessary surprise rate cut on the market late on such a day. Speculators interpreted the day's cut as meaning that Greenspan was their friend—someone who would protect them—and that they needn't really worry about the market sinking. As a result, speculation essentially became the national pastime in the ensuing 18 months.

Throughout the book, I've pointed out that the market averages kept climbing during this period, but I haven't yet detailed the speculation that was occurring. This is when events really started to spiral out of control.

The wildest and most bizarre activity took place in companies with any connection to the Internet, but anything related to technology was also fair game. Speculators tend to be attracted to ideas that have the potential for rapid growth and those that are fertile ground for their imaginations to run wild. So, it's easy to see how technology and Internet-oriented ideas got the crowd's pulse racing. What at first appeared to be maniacal behavior over time began to look tame as the bar for outlandishness kept getting set ever higher.

Over the previous few years there had been a plethora of examples of maniacal behavior, but they paled relative to what developed in late 1998 (which of course was just kid's stuff relative to what was still to come). In August 1995, jaws dropped when Netscape went public, and the stock doubled on its first day of trading. But that activity seems rather boring in comparison to the action in Theglobe.com, which went public on November 13, 1998, at $9 and closed the day at $63.50. In less time than it takes to fly across the country, the stock price had gained over 600 percent! That day the stock market briefly valued

Theglobe.com's business at over $5 billion though it only sported $2.7 million in revenues through the first three quarters of 1998. Nevertheless, its shortcomings were readily apparent, and three years later it filed for bankruptcy.

The mania notwithstanding, four days after the debut of Theglobe.com—an initial public offering (IPO) that shattered all records before and since—the revelers at the FOMC were at it again. Greenspan cut rates to 4.75 percent. They had committed the inappropriate act of cutting rates once again. The Chairman had seen fit to slash rates by a total of 75 basis points in roughly six weeks, which in turn succeeded in getting the biggest bubble of all time moving higher at an even faster pace. With this latest cut, the FOMC announced that "although conditions in financial markets had settled down materially since mid-October, unusual strains remain."

We had experienced unbridled speculation in the Internet sector; the Nasdaq 100 was up 52 percent year to date, and we'd seen total meltups in some of these narrow indexes. (For example, the SOX, the Philadelphia Semiconductor Index, was up almost 100 percent since its October lows, only six weeks earlier.) And yet the folks at the Fed were talking about unsettled conditions. At the time, a friend commented to me that Greenspan appeared to be trying to print enough money to make the consequences of his multiple errors over the decade his successor's problems. When you dig yourself into a hole, you can stop digging; but when you blow a bubble, you can't stop blowing.

As had been the case, speculation continued to intensify. The Friday after Thanksgiving, two weeks later, was a particularly memorable day. Internet-related companies saw their stock prices go berserk. Some doubled that day, while every one of the top 15 percentage-gain leaders traded on Nasdaq was up at least 45 percent! To anyone with even a modest knowledge of financial history, it was an unmistakable flashing neon sign that screamed, "reckless speculation underway." Periods such as this one had always ultimately ended in tears, just as this one did for all the day traders sprouted from this era, yet the Chairman saw nothing wrong.

Runaway stock prices and rampant speculation did not seem to alarm the FOMC. At the December 1998 meeting, Jerry Jordan, from the Cleveland Fed, made the following statement:

> I have seen—probably everyone has now seen—newsletters, advisory letters, talking heads on CNBC, and so on saying that there is no risk that the stock market is going to go down because if it even started down, the Fed would ease policy to prop it back up. So, in their view, the market can only go up from this point. I think there are more and more people coming to that belief and acting on it.

Jordan was exactly correct in his observation. In essence he told the committee precisely how the Fed was viewed by stock market speculators, describing perfectly what had come to be universally known as the Greenspan Put. However, his comment elicited *no* further discussion—it was as though he had said something as trivial as "the sky is blue"—and he said nothing more on the subject. As for the Chairman, he remained unperturbed and seemed to think he understood why stock prices were galloping higher.

At this session, Greenspan pronounced that though "security analysts have dramatically reduced their earnings expectations for the year 1998, they have not decreased their earnings expectations for the longer run. This effectively explains how the stock market can rise with earnings expectations falling."

In other words, Greenspan believed that mere *expectations*, if high enough, even though they were five years down the road, were sufficient to justify the level to which stock prices had risen. So...there was no problem with the stock market. In fact, rather than show any alarm about out-of-control speculation, he fretted that "the market could go down very substantially," in which case he was "not entirely certain how we would respond to that." If I didn't know better, I'd swear that Greenspan was trying to be humorous because there was absolutely no doubt how he would respond: *he would cut rates and print money as he had always done*.

Greenspan made one other statement worth noting: "As I've said before, a bubble is perceivable only in retrospect." Really? I'm not sure where he thought he had said it before, but this is the first evidence on the record that he had developed a new theory about bubbles. Of course his claim is pure nonsense; bubbles *are* recognizable while they are developing, just as this one was. But—and this is a big *but*—if you can't tell whether a bubble is underway or not, you can't fight it. Obviously, no one would battle against something he thought didn't exist.

Upon reflection, I'd say that Greenspan stumbled into this conclusion because he concluded that the market actually "saw" something down the road that justified its manic behavior. I feel that he believed that what the market was discounting in the future was the wondrous benefits that would accrue from his productivity thesis. Hence his explanation that there wasn't really a bubble. It never occurred to him that *his actions* caused the market to behave as it did. All of that is at least consistent; however, it does cause serious damage to Greenspan's credibility. Consider all of his comments heretofore: if he never believed there was a bubble or changed his mind about its existence, and his actions and words suggest that that is the case, why did he claim in later years (after the bubble had burst) that he tried to fight the bubble? I can only conclude he was trying to rewrite history because after the bubble collapsed, everyone, from investors to journalists, knew there had been a bubble and he could no longer pretend it hadn't existed. And since so much damage was done by its collapse, he had presumably tried to save face by claiming he attempted to prevent it.

The year 1999 saw the doors of speculation blown wide open, and it got off to a raucous start. The IPO market was on fire. According to Greg Kyle in his book *The 100 Best Internet Stocks to Own* (McGraw-Hill, 2000), the average first-day gains for companies going public were as follows: January, +271 percent; February, +145 percent; March, +146 percent; and April, +119 percent. But these numbers tell only a partial story. They don't really portray how surreal the mood of that period was. To better appreciate how bizarre the behavior was and consequently how obvious it was that a full-fledged speculative mania was underway, it is worth looking in more detail at what was happening at that time.

Many of the companies enjoying those first-day gains mentioned above were companies *in name only*; in fact, oftentimes they were no more than lavish compensation schemes for their promoters. Most had little in the way of any operating record. Quite often they had never sold a thing, and not infrequently they neither had a product to sell nor were a real business.

The Chairman obviously had trouble recognizing a bubble when he saw one, but many others sure didn't.

The clues were everywhere. For instance, there was stock-split fever; all through the late 1990s investors repeatedly chased after companies that were splitting their shares. Why? There was no good reason. If it made any economic sense, then a pizza cut into 12 slices would cost more than an identical pizza cut into only four slices. Nonetheless, the religious fervor with which stock-split candidates were lusted after was a strong hint that madness prevailed. Here is how I described that activity in my column one day in January 1999:

> Here's an interesting development. Broadcast.com (BCST) was up about 95 points when it was halted. The Nasdaq asked the company for comments about why the stock was up as much as it was, but the company said it didn't have anything to say about that. It's breathtaking when you see a stock trading at $230 per share, up $95 on the day.

The next day I wrote:

> The company [Broadcast.com], which had nothing to say about the stock's moon shot previously, decided to divulge that it was planning a two for one stock split. That made it good for another 87 points, which in turn, ignited all of the net stocks—YHOO up 72 points, Go2Net up 54, Mindspring and Ink-tomi both up 22. Amazon was a laggard, up only 24.

A couple of months later, I attempted to put into perspective the amount of money that was being assigned to the benefits of this paper shuffling that had no financial meaning:

> Today, we have the happy event of Microsoft's (MSFT) long-awaited split. There are now over 5.6 billion fully diluted shares of Microsoft outstanding, and the price is approaching $100, yet all the splitsters are probably looking for the next split. To put these big numbers in perspective, today's $3 move in Microsoft adds approximately the same value as one year's worth of revenues [about $18 billion at the time] to its market capitalization. Microsoft's valuation now equals about $530 billion, which is approximately six percent of the gross domestic product of the U.S.A.

Then there was the behavior of the Wall Street "analysts" who would later be unmasked as the shills that they were. They did not try to explain why, based on their in-depth analysis, a company was a compelling investment. Their modus operandi was just to raise their target price for a stock, which would cause it to take off like a scalded dog. Then, when that target price was reached, the analysts would do it all over again. The other trick in their analytical bag was to explain why if XYZinternetgiveaway.com fetched one price, it meant that some other companies could be worth more too. So when other stocks traded higher, that meant still others were then entitled to move higher as well. Buy recommendations made by analysts created action that fueled investor optimism and fanned the flames of speculation. The Land of Make Believe, however, is a very large place, and we had explored only a tiny part of it relative to what was yet to come.

Still, you didn't really have to look too far or be too smart to see that we were in the midst of a speculative bubble that was completely out of control. You didn't, that is, unless your name was Alan Greenspan.

To Greenspan, it all made sense. In a speech on May 6, 1999, to the Federal Reserve Bank of Chicago's 35th Annual Conference on Bank Structure and Competition, he explained:

> This view is reinforced by securities analysts who presumably are knowledgeable about the companies they follow. This veritable army of technicians has been projecting increasingly higher five-year earnings growth, on average, since early 1995.... There appears little reason to doubt that analysts' continuous upward revisions reflect what companies are reporting to them about improved cost control, which on a consolidated basis for the economy

overall, adds up to accelerating labor productivity.… Thus, companies are apparently conveying to analysts that, to date, they see no diminution in expectations of productivity acceleration. This does not mean that the analysts are correct, or for that matter the companies, only that what companies are evidently telling the analysts about their productivity and profits are doubtless reflected in the longer-term profit projections. The macroeconomic data to date certainly suggest little evidence of a slowdown in productivity growth.

Once again Greenspan was able to rationalize the maniacal behavior that took place daily. Productivity explained it all. Companies felt good, analysts felt good—all was well because productivity was powering a new era. His predecessor at the Fed, Paul Volcker, the man who had successfully broken the back of inflation in the early 1980s, didn't quite see it that way. He had too much respect for his former office and was too much of a gentleman to be direct, yet on May 14, 1999, he made the following point in a commencement address to the American University, School of Public Affairs/Kogod School of Business: "The fate of the world economy is now totally dependent on the growth of the U.S. economy, which is dependent on the stock market, whose growth is dependent on about 50 stocks, half of which have never reported any earnings."

In his own understated way, Volcker had just served notice that a bubble was in full bloom. The tail was wagging the dog. The stock market was valued at 180 percent of gross domestic product (GDP), over 100 percent higher than the 85 percent of GDP it reached during the last bubble in 1929. (See Figure 4 on page 69.)

Volcker saw it; Greenspan didn't.

By now Greenspan was really tap dancing, concluding that it was exceedingly difficult to spot a bubble in the making. On June 17, 1999, he told Congress: "Bubbles generally are perceptible only after the fact. To spot a bubble in advance requires a judgment that hundreds of thousands of informed investors have it all wrong. Betting against markets is usually precarious at best."

Really? Where did this come from? That's exactly what bubbles are all about—a crowd gone mad. And, a crowd that had gotten it all wrong.

These *informed investors* he refers to behaved as they did because Greenspan acted as he did. They were a reflection of his policies. The fact that there were "hundreds of thousands of them" did not mean you could only recognize it "after the fact." This was just another excuse Greenspan concocted as to why there couldn't be a bubble when in fact it should have been obvious to anyone with an understanding of human nature and financial history that one was deeply entrenched and expanding rapidly.

By late August 1999, the Nasdaq had doubled from its October 1998 low and the Fed had just raised rates for

Molly Evans

Figure 4 The Consequences of the Maestro's Easy Money Policies

the second time to 5.25 percent. This action in light of what was occurring was quite cowardly. *The Economist*, the well-respected British magazine, opined:

> [A] prudent central bank would have tightened policy more aggressively by now. Yet even after this week's rise, American short-term interest rates are still a quarter of a point lower than they were a year ago…. [S]uch timid moves may falsely reassure Wall Street that the Fed has everything safely under control—encouraging the stock market to ever-giddier heights…. But… [Greenspan's] dilemma is largely of his own making: it reflects a failure to tackle America's economic imbalances earlier, before they had become so severe.

At the FOMC meeting on November 16, 1999—yet another one in which the word *bubble* was never uttered—the Fed finally removed the last of the 75 basis point easing it had deemed necessary the prior fall, raising rates to 5.50 percent. However, although the cost of borrowing was being raised a bit, the Fed was about to force-feed the banking system with mountains of money as it fretted over the chaos that might ensue when the world's digital clocks made the transition to the year 2000. That poorly handled and ultimately totally unnecessary liquidity injection blew the top off the stock market as it made one final burst higher.

Chapter 4

Bubbleonians Running the Asylum: The Bubble Blow-Off
(1999–2000)

The stock market bubble, fueled by wild enthusiasm for technology and especially Internet stocks, explodes higher ... Greenspan has brought America to the promised land of the New Economy. The Fed prints money, keeps rates low, and blows the roof off the stock market with its Y2K liquidity injections. IPOs are king, and there is seemingly no limit to how high stock prices will go. Prosperity reigns supreme. But it is all just a mirage.

Hey there, Mr. Greenspan, you don't scare us. We're the stock market and we're ready for whatever you and your colleagues decide to dish out, so go ahead and take your best shot. If you decide to raise interest rates next week, that's fine. We can deal with it. And should you think it's unnecessary to boost rates, that's even better. In other words—whatever you and your band of merry central bankers decide to do on Nov. 16 is OK with the stock market....

While economists, Fed watchers, and the media are obsessing over whether or not you will hike rates come the 16th, read our lips—it really doesn't matter what you do. Here's the reason: If you should decide to raise the federal funds rate by a quarter of a point, that would only bring it back to where it was on Sept. 30 of last year, before you cut it three times, a quarter of a point each time. No big deal. At 5.5 percent, this was not an impediment to rising stock prices; equities had a pretty good year in 1998, you will recall.

Besides, you're not going to raise rates again for the rest of this century. Indeed, we're willing to wager that you won't even be thinking about a rate hike until spring in the new millennium—if then. Care to know why? Because you've already told us that you plan to inject some $50 billion extra into the financial system to help tide the banks over any cash needs they might have arising from their customers' concerns over Y2K.[1] It wouldn't make sense to put money in with one hand and take it out with the other, would it?… Yes, Mr. Greenspan, we're going to start our New Year's party early no matter what you do on the 16th. It's called exuberance: get used to it.

The November 1999 rate hike to 5.50 percent was a nonevent as far as speculators were concerned. It had no impact. It was tiny and overshadowed by the Fed's Y2K liquidity infusion. More importantly, they had already figured out that the Fed was no threat to them. The mood was so out of control at that time that I felt I could no longer describe it adequately and relied on actual examples of madness from real people that would come my way. I included many in my columns and dubbed the vignettes "The Mania Chronicles." The first one, featured above, appeared on November 9, 1999, having originally been posted on the CBS Market Watch site by its author, Dr. Irwin Kellner. It was an absolutely perfect illustration of how Bubbleonians[2] viewed the Fed.

My column on November 10, 1999, contained a small sample of what that New Year's party looked like, describing how groups of stocks gaining 10 to 20 percent were an everyday occurrence—and these were all companies with $5 billion to $20 billion market caps, most of which hadn't even existed 18 months prior to that time. Remember the monster moves of that era? Here's a snapshot of that day—Liberate Technology up about $34, a mere 50 percent move; Next Level Communications up $31, about a 150 percent move; and iBasis Technology, up $24, a 150+ percent gain. When the bubble deflated, those stocks each declined by over 90 percent.

Between September 20 and November 10, 1999, the Fed had printed enough money to explode the broad aggregate of the money supply by $147 billion, which was an annualized growth rate of 14.3 percent. In fact, this money printing went a long way toward explaining the bubble itself. From February 1996 through October 1999, the money supply, according to one measure, expanded by about $1.6 trillion, or 20 percent of GDP. At that rate, the money supply would double every eight years.

It's quite easy to see why the November 16 rate hike was laughed off by the Bubbleonians. The result of the Fed pumping money into the system to ease Y2K fears, coming on the heels of four years of straight up markets that appeared to have no risk, combined with belief in the Greenspan Put, produced an out-of-control frenzy. IPOs were routinely leaping by staggering amounts on the first day—if not in the first hours—of trading. Cobalt Network jumped 482 percent, Foundry Network was good for 525 percent, Akamai Technologies soared 458 percent. And so it went. The valuations were so absurd as to be nearly meaningless—all three of those companies were trading in excess of 100 times *sales*. This meant that if you bought the entire business and the sales generated incurred no expenses, it would take you 100 years to get your money back, give or take, depending on how fast the company's revenues grew.

But the IPO Leaper Award had to go to VA Linux, which skyrocketed 681 percent on December 15, 1999. Fred Hickey, editor of the highly regarded *High Tech Strategist* newsletter, described the delirious state of mind of the Bubbleonians this way:

> Virtually any company with dot.com in its name can get funding to start a business. It seems that entrepreneurs are running out of ideas for new dot.com companies; we're now into the ridiculous stage. Part of Route 128 in Massachusetts is sponsored by FreeLotto.com. Great idea. Pay nothing for lottery tickets and still win money. Mypoints.com, beenz.com and Surfbuzz.com will reward surfers [visitors] visiting their sites with coupons or bonus points that are used to buy computers, vacations, and the like. Alladvantage.com, ePipe.com and GoToWorld.com are promising to pay cash for the time you spend online. YouNetwork is giving away shares of stock. These something-for-nothing stock sites are trying to establish business models where they will theoretically garner revenues from advertisers for the "eyeballs" they've captured. The real intent is to get enough "eyeballs" to justify an IPO, and then dump the shares on the unwitting public.[3]

The IPO action was so loony that even someone at the Fed noticed. At the December 21 FOMC meeting, Fed staffer Mike Prell observed:

> To illustrate the speculative character of the market, let me cite an excerpt from a recent IPO prospectus: "We incurred losses of $14.5 million in fiscal 1999 primarily due to expansion of our operations, and we had an accumulated deficit of $15.0 million as of July 31, 1999. We expect to continue to incur significant expenses, particularly as a result of expanding our direct sales force.... We do not expect to generate sufficient revenues to achieve profitability and, therefore, we expect to continue to incur net losses for at least the foreseeable future. If we do achieve profitability, we may not be able to sustain it." Based on these prospects, the VA Linux IPO [Author's note: which was the IPO leaper just described] recorded a first-day price gain of about 700 percent and has a market cap of roughly $9 billion. Not bad for a company that some analysts say has no hold on any significant technology.

Prell then compared the millennium stock market to one of the most famous bubbles of all time: the South Sea bubble that consumed France and England around 1720.

The warning language I've just read is at least an improvement in disclosure compared to the classic prospectus of the South Sea Bubble era, in which someone offered shares in "a company for carrying on an undertaking of great advantage, but nobody to know what it is." [Prell wondered] "whether the spirit of the times isn't becoming similar to that of the earlier period."

He then described how impervious speculators were to the Fed's rate hikes:

Earlier this year, those stocks supposedly were damaged when rates rose, because, people said, quite logically, that the present values of their distant earnings were greatly affected by the rising discount factor. At this point, those same *people are abandoning all efforts at fundamental analysis and talking about momentum as the only thing that matters.*" [italics mine]

And then Prell zeroed in on the real danger:

If this speculation were occurring on a scale that wasn't lifting the overall market, it might be of concern only for the distortions in resource allocation it might be causing. But it has in fact been *giving rise to significant gains in household wealth and thereby contributing to the rapid growth of consumer demand*—something reflected in the internal and external saving imbalances that are much discussed in some circles." [italics mine]

Eureka! Finally, someone at the Fed saw that a dangerous bubble was well underway. Sadly, Prell's totally accurate assessment of the environment fell on deaf ears. Not one member of the FOMC—including the Chairman—bothered to ask Prell a single question about what he had described. He may as well have read them his grocery list.

As for Y2K, the fear about what terrible developments might trip up the financial system when clocks changed to the year 2000, which caused the Fed to explode the monetary base by an annualized rate of 44 percent over the last 10 weeks of the year—it was essentially treated as a nonevent by the FOMC. Amazingly, after all that money printing, no Fed governor expressed any real angst about it, but several thought it was a yawner. Ed Boehne said, "The report from bankers around the District is that they believe that Y2K will be a nonevent. They have lots of cash in their vaults but few customers requesting unusually large withdrawals." Cathy Minehan saw a variation of the same thing: "It is hard to find any Y2K panic or even deep worries out there, and believe me we've tried to find it." Bill Poole was even less perturbed: "I'm guessing that at the end of the day we will find virtually all of this Y2K effect lost in the rounding error and we are not going to see much effect."

And optimism flowed forth…no one was worried. Here, they had printed all of this money to save U.S. citizens from a nonproblem without taking any action whatsoever (for example, raising margin requirements) that might have at least prevented the final six-month blow-off in the mania. At this final meeting of the century, the biggest challenge that Y2K seemed to present to the Chairman was how to word the committee's communiqué: "The crucial issue for this meeting, as Don Kohn very clearly pointed out, is to recognize that we have a Y2K problem. It is a problem about which we do not want to become complacent and presume that it doesn't matter." You might think he was actually concerned about Y2K itself, but a reading of the transcript shows that Greenspan's really big worry was whether the Fed should tell the world that its bias regarding future rate hikes was "symmetrical" or "asymmetrical." Their deliberations show just how much faith they put in their own jawboning as they haggled endlessly over the two choices. In the end, symmetry won, meaning that the Fed had no predisposition either way regarding its likely course of action.

At the end of the millennium, the price/earnings ratio of the Nasdaq Index was estimated to be approximately

200, with that index having appreciated 907 percent in the prior five years. In the late 1980s Japan experienced a large bubble that had many investors at the time shaking their heads in disbelief. Their speculative mania seems quite tame by comparison, as the price/earnings ratio for the Japanese stock market index, the Nikkei, topped out around 80, while the last five years of appreciation was an almost modest sounding 230 percent.

On January 3, 2000, I penned a column in which Chairman Greenspan was anointed Dot.com Dad—the father of Internet speculation. Here's the explanation of why I named him that:

About this time last year [in early 1999] when Internet speculation was just getting rolling, Greenspan was busy putting liquidity into the system. As liquidity was jammed in all year, it had to go somewhere and it went to the places where there were the fewest fundamentals, and the most imagination—that is, Internet stocks. That's the way speculation often works; it seeks ideas with the highest imagination potential and fewest hard facts. Greenspan fueled all sorts of Internet ideas no matter how risky or kooky— all year long, and then of course, we hit the afterburners late in the year. The price of Internet stocks went so high, so fast and made some folks so much money, that people concluded, by God, there must be something to the Internet. As a result, Internet entrepreneurs were deemed to be visionaries who had read the *Wall Street Journal* for the year 2020 and were telling us what the future would look like.

My belief then was that Greenspan, through his irresponsible monetary policy, had fomented massive speculation that drove Internet stock prices to such high levels that they were completely incomprehensible. Those high prices, the wealth that accrued to the owners of those shares, and the confidence that wealth brought with it convinced people that they knew what the future looked like. In reality, no one at the time knew how the Internet madness would sort out. (An interesting aside pertaining to that period: later in 2000, a survey was taken by the National Academy of Engineers which asked its members to rank the greatest engineering feats of the twentieth century. Out of the 20 accomplishments listed, the Internet was ranked thirteenth, behind electricity, automobiles, airplanes, computers, telephones, and spacecraft.[4]) As the bubble roared on, Greenspan seemed to become even more infatuated with technology, its impact on productivity, and the possibility that we had entered some sort of a new era. Adding to the frenzy, the *Wall Street Journal* was taken in by all the excitement as well and saw fit to call this era the "New Economy."

On January 13, 2000, Greenspan gave the first variation of a speech he would give over and over again that year. It was titled "Technology and the Economy." In this particular speech, Greenspan wondered out loud how history would view this period:

> When we look back at the 1990s, from the perspective of say 2010, the nature of the forces currently in train will have presumably become clearer. We may conceivably conclude from that vantage point that, at the turn of the millennium, the American economy was experiencing a once-in-a-century acceleration of innovation, which propelled forward productivity, output, corporate profits, and stock prices at a pace not seen in generations, if ever.
>
> Alternatively, that 2010 retrospective might well conclude that a good deal of what we are currently experiencing was just one of the many euphoric speculative bubbles that have dotted human history. And, of course, we cannot rule out that we may look back and conclude that elements from both scenarios have been in play in recent years.
>
> On the one hand, the evidence of dramatic innovations—veritable shifts in the tectonic plates of technology—has moved far beyond mere conjecture. On the other, these extraordinary achievements continue to be bedeviled by concerns that the so-called New Economy is spurring imbalances that at some point will abruptly adjust, bringing the

economic expansion, its euphoria, and wealth creation to a debilitating halt.

Greenspan then proceeded to throw his weight behind the former conclusion: "But it is information technology that defines this special period. The reason is that information innovation lies at the root of productivity and economic growth. Its major contribution is to reduce the number of worker hours required to produce the nation's output."

He further explained why technology was the *secret sauce* in the process: "Before this revolution in information availability, most twentieth-century business decision making had been hampered by wide uncertainty.... Indeed, these developments emphasize the essence of information technology—the expansion of knowledge and its obverse, the reduction in uncertainty."

The Chairman next explained how screaming stock prices were *just rewards* for those taking the risk of capital investment: "Had high prospective returns on these capital projects not materialized, the current capital equipment investment boom—there is no better word—would have petered out long ago.... To be sure, there is also a virtuous capital investment cycle at play here. A whole new set of profitable investments raises productivity, which for a time raises profits—spurring further investment and consumption." In other words we had damn near achieved nirvana.

Greenspan wound up his case in a summation of how this interrelated process even made the economy grow faster (which it did, but in a misallocated way, not in the wondrous manner he envisioned):

But in recent years, largely as a result of the appreciating values of ownership claims on the capital stock [Author's note: that is, escalating stock prices], themselves a consequence, at least in part, of accelerating productivity, the net worth of households has expanded dramatically, relative to income. This has spurred private consumption to rise even faster than the incomes engendered by the productivity-driven rise in output growth. Moreover, the fall in the cost of equity capital corresponding to higher share prices, coupled with enhanced potential rates of return, has spurred private capital investment.

Greenspan was making the case for a new era, yet he was careful not to actually utter those words himself. As for the possibility of the other outcome, that this was "just one of the many euphoric speculative bubbles," he didn't build a case for that, which is not surprising. However, he notes that "what will stop the wealth-induced excess of demand over productivity-expanded supply is largely developments in financial markets. That process is already well advanced." He then backpedaled by stating that "for the equity wealth effect to be contained, either expected future earnings must decline, or the discount factor applied to those earnings must rise. There is little evidence of the former. Indeed, security analysts, reflecting detailed information on and from the companies they cover, have continued to revise *upward* long-term earnings projections." Greenspan went on to explain that the rise in longer-term interest rates ("the discount factor applied to those earnings") was "quite natural." In any case, Bubble-onians need not have worried about declining stock prices because "a diminution of the wealth effect... does not mean that prices of assets cannot keep rising, only that they rise no more than income." Translation: the worst case, folks, is that stock prices will rise at a slower rate.

Despite its prior symmetrical directive, the Fed raised interest rates one-quarter of 1 percentage point to 5.75 percent on February 2, 2000. (Interest rates were now back to where they had been almost five years earlier in July 1995.) Though the FOMC bumped rates a bit higher, they did so due to inflation fears—price inflation, not asset (that is, bubble) inflation. The stock market was unperturbed. That week the Nasdaq blasted off to its biggest weekly gain in roughly 25 years: 9 percent. A week after the rate hike, Cisco reported its quarterly results. My column from that day provides a useful snap-shot of just how much investors shared the Chairman's love affair with technology:

> Cisco reported a fine quarter and predictably the stock went berserk. At one point, Cisco was up nearly $10. At that moment it would have been valued at over 150 times earnings and over 40 times revenues. Cisco added to its market capital-ization three years' worth of revenues. Was the quarter that great?
>
> **How high is too high?**... It begs the question of how many points are too many. Can a stock ever reach too high a price? Bubblevision [CNBC] was discussing that Cisco might be the first company to hit a trillion-dollar market cap. Well, in this mania anything's possible. [Author's note: Cisco's market capitalization at the time was approximately $500 billion.] But, folks, the whole world's GDP is only slightly above $30 trillion. Can a company with $12 billion in revenues—or even $15 billion or $20 bil-lion—really be worth a trillion dollars, 3 percent of world GDP? U.S. GDP is only $9 trillion, so could one company with that amount of revenues be worth one-tenth of the U.S. economy? When we look back on this, those are the kinds of big num-bers that will cause people to say, "How did anyone ever think those things were possible?"

One factor that drove prices higher was the explosive increase in margin debt, something that the Fed was specifically empowered to affect. The Securities and Exchange Act of 1934 delegated to the Fed the power to regulate broker loans—also known as "margin debt"—used to purchase stocks. The rules at the time, as they had been for 25 years, allowed speculators to borrow up to 50 percent of the value of their stock purchases. As of February 2000, total margin debt stood at $265 billion. *It had grown 45 percent since the previous October and had more than tripled since the end of 1995.* Relative to GDP, margin debt was the highest it had been since 1929, and over three times as high as it was in October 1987. It was an unmistakable sign of rampant speculation.

On February 17, 2000, the subject of margin debt came up when the Chairman testified before the House Banking Committee, just as it had three weeks earlier when Greenspan had appeared before the same committee in the Senate. Despite having been thoroughly interrogated on the subject by an obviously concerned Senator Charles Schumer on January 26, Greenspan reiterated the view that he shared in his previous testimony, that raising margin requirements would have no effect on stock prices.

In response to questions from Senator Schumer during that January Senate appearance, Greenspan had staked out his views on the subject, stating that raising margin requirements would discriminate against the small investor and, furthermore, studies had "suggested that the level of stock prices has nothing to do with margin requirements."

I have *no idea* what studies he was referring to; there was no such study discussed in any FOMC meeting. Perhaps he was referring to the lone paper on the subject available at the Fed's Web site, written on April 22, 1997, by Paul Kupiec, titled "Margin Requirements, Volatility and Market Integrity: What Have We Learned Since the Crash?" He may have felt Kupiec's paper in and of itself said all that there was to say on the subject. Nonetheless, it was not a topic of discussion at FOMC meetings. Furthermore, there were plenty of examples that suggested that the Chairman's view of the effectiveness of raising margin requirements was not shared by others in a position of regulatory supervision. The various futures exchanges routinely raised margin requirements to cool off speculation and protect the integrity of the exchange. In fact, just two days before Greenspan's Senate appearance, the New York Mercantile Exchange raised the margin requirements, effective immediately, on heating oil by 80 percent.

Incredibly, Greenspan also told the Senator that the Fed was well aware of the margin numbers, that they had "moved up at a pace which has created a good deal of evaluation on our part and obviously other supervisory regulators, and there's been considerable conversation going on with respect to addressing this issue because it goes beyond the mere issue of stocks." The considerable conversation apparently did *not* take place at FOMC meetings, however, as the transcripts do not include discussions on the subject. Nor was Senator Schumer persuaded by Greenspan's arguments, because two days after that hearing he asked Senator Phil Gramm, the Senate Banking Committee chairman, to conduct hearings on the subject of margin debt.

On March 6, 2000, the Chairman attended a New Economy conference at Boston College where he strutted his own New Economy credentials with the following distillation of the economic and financial landscape: "The fact that the capital spending boom is still growing strong indicates that businesses continue to find a wide array of potential high-rate-of-return, productivity-enhancing investments. And I see nothing to suggest that these opportunities will peter out any time soon. Indeed, many argue that the pace of innovation will continue to quicken in the next few years, as companies exploit the still largely untapped potential for e-commerce...." Four days later the Nasdaq would peak out at 5048, from which it would ultimately decline 84 percent in the ensuing 30 months. But that was a fact no one knew at the time. Speculation was at fever pitch. In the weeks surrounding that market top, my daily column routinely featured Mania Chronicle vignettes detailing various forms of out-of-control behavior. The one I dubbed "the most sensational so far" occurred just days before the Nasdaq peak:

A friend of mine who is a computer software consultant has decided not to pay his quarterly taxes to the Feds and is putting it into the market instead. He says the penalty is only nine percent and he can beat that easily in the stock market. He has it all in Rambus (RMBS). It should be an interesting ride from now to April 15. Wonder how many other people are doing this?

That fairy tale didn't have a happy ending, as the price of a share of Rambus declined nearly 50 percent by tax time. Many people would learn the hard way that speculating was fun while it worked, yet could be disastrous when it didn't. But enormous numbers of people didn't even know that they *were* speculating. They were lambs led to the slaughter. Few at the time seemed to worry about the consequences of all the speculation and the misallocation of capital taking place. Oh, sure, there were a handful of us critics speaking out, but no one in any position of power tried very hard to emphasize the risks.

Certainly not Alan Greenspan.

Chapter 5

The Stock Bubble Bursts: The Tech Miracle Was a Mirage
(2000–2001)

The year 2000 turned tragic for investors who sank their savings into technology stocks. The tech boom implodes, but Greenspan doesn't see it. He sticks to the promise of productivity growth and continues his love affair with technology throughout 2000.

I'm writing with a heavy heart and tears in my eyes. I have worked hard all of my life, always trying to do the right thing for my family, friends and the world in general. I have never taken advantage of another person in any way. I have scrimped and saved over the years, as I did not have the luxury of a company pension or retirement plan. When I became aware of CYBR [Cyber Care Inc.], I did voluminous amounts of research and only after I was totally convinced, I started buying. I admit that I probably got caught up in all of the good repartee being bantered about the boards and violated some of my own basic rules of investing, but I really believed and, in fact, still do.

I have literally lost everything I have worked for my entire lifetime. A woman whose husband bought into CYBR on my recommendation called me this morning in tears, as she thinks her husband is going to kill himself, as he followed my advice. We are both 62 years old and cannot recover from this....

I did make a giant mistake by buying on margin. I have had to liquidate shares several times for margin calls and thought that the nightmare was finally over. Then this week happened. I am now so far in the hole that even if I liquidate totally, I still owe! Now, that's incredible and shows the dangers of margin. I have until tomorrow and I don't know what to do, other than hope for a miracle....

Now, after enduring all of the pain of the last few months, I won't be able to share in the final rewards. I even took a second mortgage in March to pay [my] margin [debt] down, so strong was my belief in this company. Now that money is gone, too. So instead of looking forward to a nice retirement, I will have to hope I keep my health and am able to keep on working. This is a hard fact to swallow.

I have been through a lot of troubles in my lifetime, but I can honestly tell you that today is, without question, the worst day of my life. I wish all of you well.

This incredibly tragic tale from the spring of 2000 was forwarded to me by a regular reader of my daily column. This man's tale was not unique. There would be countless financial horror stories told as the stock market collapsed over the next three years.

The FOMC meeting on March 21, 2000, was quite similar to all those just prior to it. The term "stock market" is mentioned at least 20 times in the transcripts from that particular meeting, but not with any sense of alarm. Several committee members noted the unusual *correlation*, or lack thereof, between the Nasdaq and the Dow Jones Industrial Average. The chatter about the Nasdaq versus the Dow was mostly an intellectual exercise and stimulated no serious discussion. However, Cathy Minehan from the Boston Fed relayed a very important conversation she had with a contact of hers who told her that:

> …in her experience, CEOs of major firms across the nation are now more concerned about the stock market than they ever have been. She noted that this phenomenon goes well beyond stocks and stock options that they might receive as compensation. Senior managers seem to look at the stock market as the ultimate arbiter of success and they spend time—time that in earlier periods might have been spent solely focused on the business—on financial engineering related to the price level of their company's stock. It was an interesting conversation because it seemed to suggest that today's period of stock market ebullience has similarities to the period of the late '70s and early '80s, when inflationary excesses affected corporate and consumer decision making.

This anecdote perfectly fits the definition of a bubble given by John Makin of the American Enterprise Institute: "A stock market bubble exists when the value of stocks has more impact on the economy than the economy has on the value of stocks."[1]

Minehan drew only one comment from the meeting's attendees on her observation, and it created no discussion.

Meanwhile Greenspan had nothing to say about stock prices other than to comment on the issue of the unusual relationship between the indices that had been raised by others:

> Indeed, one possible explanation for the remarkable performance of the Nasdaq in relation to the Dow—this extraordinary negative correlation that Bill Poole [Author's note: one of the FOMC members who made this point] put his finger on—is that we have in the market's evaluation process for existing capital a clear indication that capital is moving out of the older technologies into the new.

Greenspan did have a firm grasp of the obvious as far as where the hot money was headed, but he apparently had no idea that *he* was one of the primary reasons why it was happening. Still, Greenspan was generally sanguine as he defaulted to one of his favorite areas of comfort. "So as far as I can judge just looking at the data, it is not evident that we are seeing, as yet, a cresting in the growth of productivity." Again, the word *bubble* was never uttered in this session, nor were the words *margin requirements* mentioned by anyone.

As I noted earlier, technology can be a powerful aphrodisiac. It certainly had its way with the Chairman; it blinded him to the bubble that should have been obvious to anyone.

Approximately two weeks later, on April 7, 2000, Greenspan delivered a speech once again extolling the virtues of investing in new technology. It was a seminal speech for the Chairman—a tribute to the technology gods delivered at the top of the bubble. It merits serious examination; in it Greenspan makes it extremely clear exactly how he viewed the world:

> When historians look back at the latter half of the 1990s a decade or two hence, I suspect that they will conclude we are now living through a pivotal period in American economic history. New technologies that evolved from the cumulative innovations of the past half-century have now begun to bring about dramatic changes in the way goods and services are produced and in the way they are distributed to final users. Those innovations, exemplified most recently by the multiplying uses of the Internet, have brought on a flood of start-up firms, many of which claim to offer the chance to revolutionize and dominate large shares of the nation's production and distribution system.... [Author's note: Greenspan demonstrates that he apparently doesn't understand cause and effect. The start-ups were a response to the bubble, not a response to the technology.]
>
> By the 1990s, these and a number of lesser but critical innovations had, in turn, fostered an enormous new capacity to capture, analyze, and dissem-

inate information. It is the growing use of information technology throughout the economy that makes the current period unique. [Author's note: Actually, it was the massive bubble that made it unique.]

However, until the mid-1990s, the billions of dollars that businesses had poured into information technology seemed to leave little imprint on the overall economy. The investment in new technology arguably had not yet cumulated to be a sizable part of the U.S. capital stock, and computers were still being used largely on a stand-alone basis. The full value of computing power could be realized only after ways had been devised to link computers into large-scale networks. [Author's note: Greenspan is trying to make the case that it was only networking that made technology really useful, and we only recently reached that point. That is a difficult conclusion to support, since networking had been around in various forms for over a decade. What's more, plenty of technologies such as fax machines or cell phones worked just fine un-networked. The imprint on the economy that he notes is actually the imprint of the bubble.]

By 1995 the investment boom had gathered momentum, suggesting that earlier expectations of elevated profitability had not been disappointed. In that year, with inflation falling, domestic operating profit margins started to rise, indicating that increases

in unit costs were slowing. These developments sig-
naled that productivity growth was probably beginning to move higher, even though official data,
hobbled by statistical problems, failed to provide any
confirmation. Now, five years later, there can be little doubt that not only has productivity growth
picked up from its rather tepid pace during the pre-
ceding quarter-century, but that the growth rate has
continued to rise, with scant evidence that it is about
to crest.

[Author's note: The year 1995 was when things
changed; Greenspan is correct to note that as an
inflection point. However, as we have seen, the
post-1995 stock market action was a function of
Greenspan's actions at the Fed, which powered the
bubble, which, in turn, fueled the investment
boom. He couldn't see the bubble because he had
decided that technology's impact on productivity
explained why the stock market had gone wild.]

Greenspan never said we were in a new era, but it sure
seemed as though he was pretty darn sympathetic to the
idea. At the top of the bubble, his statements indicate
that he didn't realize that he had just presided over the
biggest stock market bubble this country had ever seen.

A week later, on April 13, 2000, when the Chairman
was in front of the Senate Banking Committee, he was
asked if an interest rate hike would prick the stock market

bubble. He responded: "That presupposes I know that there is a bubble.... I don't think we can know there's been a bubble until after the fact. To assume we know it currently presupposes that we have the capacity to forecast an imminent decline in prices." The man was telling the truth when he said he didn't know "that there is a bubble." The facts, in the form of FOMC meeting transcripts and speeches, back up his claim. Of course, those same facts and his response that day are a bit inconvenient for Greenspan today, given what he would later say about his actions during the bubble years. We looked earlier at many of Greenspan's claims about his years heading the Fed, but I think one bears reviewing again now. In Chapter 1, I shared his quote from 2006 when Greenspan said, "We didn't ease until 2001 because we wanted to be certain the bubble was over." That statement is clearly wrong. He didn't believe there was a bubble in 2000, so there was no reason to wait to ease until he was "certain" it was over.

So, why did Greenspan wait to ease? For the same reason—because he didn't know there had been a bubble; so he didn't know what its bursting would mean. Eventually enough damage would become evident that he would respond to it, but that would not happen until 2001.

At the FOMC meeting on May 16, 2000, the Fed hiked interest rates by half a percent to 6.5 percent, though that would be the last hike for four years. The transcript of that meeting is much the same as the others we have reviewed. Mike Prell sounded the alarms that the "speculative bubble [was] of extraordinary proportions." As had been the case with his earlier warning, this one too fell on deaf ears. (See pages 76–78.) During that early summer meeting, Greenspan used the term "stock market" just once but only in passing. He did, however, opt to raise rates a half a percentage point because "the evidence indicates that productivity, indeed perhaps [even] underlying GDP, is still accelerating." The Chairman said confidently, "I think the underlying momentum in the economy remains very strong."

The stock market bubble, which had exhausted itself in early March, was taking no prisoners as it slid. The Nasdaq peaked at 5048 on March 10, 2000 (24 percent higher for the year as of that day), and stood at 3164 on May 23, 2000. By that point in time, the index was down 23 percent for the year and a staggering 47 percent from the highs. A great deal of damage was done in those 10 weeks.

Real people, like the individual whose story opened this chapter, felt real pain as the bubble deflated. Some had only themselves to blame, while others were hurt who did not participate in the bubble, yet suffered during the ensuing recession. Of course, nearly everyone would have fared better had Greenspan and the Fed behaved more responsibly. In the years after the stock market crash of 1929, many rules were changed to protect investors. Greenspan was so confident in his understanding of the economy and markets that he apparently didn't give prior speculative manias, or this one, any real weight in his analysis. Consequently, rather than try to prevent the bubble, he was forced to attempt to clean up the mess that was left in its aftermath.

Those May lows would hold until November. In the interim, the Chairman, oblivious as he was to the unfolding storm, continued to repeat the same sort of speeches about the economy and productivity. On June 13, 2000, in a speech titled "Business Data Analysis," Greenspan stated: "That there has been some underlying improvement in the growth of aggregate productivity is now generally conceded by all but the most skeptical." He misread his critics. It wasn't that they didn't believe in productivity. Quite the opposite—they did. They just felt that the data were being tortured in such a way that the Fed's view of productivity and everything that flowed from its calculation were overstated. As it turned out, Greenspan's critics were right to approach the Fed's emphasis on productivity with a certain amount of reservation; many of Greenspan's claims regarding the productivity miracle were exaggerated.

James Grant, editor of the always insightful *Grant's Interest Rate Observer*, was one skeptic who took the trouble to dissect the complicated subject that Greenspan seemed to accept at face value. In the spring of 2000, Grant publicized a study by Robert J. Gordon, a Northwestern University economics professor, who had prepared for the Congressional Budget Office a paper with a shocking revelation:

> There has been no productivity growth acceleration in the 99% of the economy located outside the sector which manufactures computer hardware.... Indeed, far from exhibiting a productivity acceleration, the productivity slowdown in manufacturing has gotten worse: when computers are stripped out of the durable manufacturing sector, there has been a further productivity slowdown in durable manufacturing in 1995–99 as compared to 1972–95, and no acceleration at all in nondurable manufacturing.

Grant backed that thunderbolt up with another study conducted by two economists, James Medoff and Andrew Harless. Their contention was that the use of a hedonic price index grossly misrepresented the actual data. (Hedonics adjustments and how they are misleading were discussed in Chapter 2.)

Grant described what you see in Figure 5 this way:

> The top line, bearing a close resemblance to a high-tech stock chart, divides the computer industry's output (using the hedonic calculation) by hours worked; it conveys the familiar, almost miraculous,

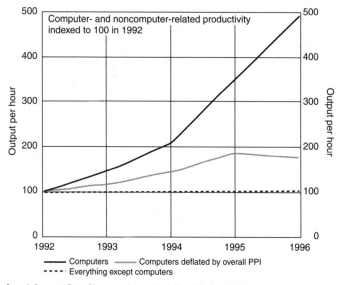

Grant's Interest Rate Observer; James Medoff and Andrew Harless

Figure 5 Productivity: A Statistical Phenomenon

productivity story. The middle line also measures productivity in the computer industry, but omits the hedonic calculation; instead, the overall Producer Price Index (PPI) is used to arrive at the real value of computer industry production. Productivity growth in this case is positive, but something less than inspirational. The bottom line describes productivity growth in every industry except computers. As Gordon discovered, it goes absolutely nowhere.

The economists then explained why the potential existed for erroneous conclusions:

In principle, a flawed application of the hedonic pricing methodology could result in a bias in either direction. In recent U.S. data [circa spring 2000], the direction of bias is clear: the rate of decline in computer prices is being exaggerated, as rapid introductions of new technology are interpreted as large declines in the price of existing technology. Modest growth in the dollar value of hardware and software produced is reported as awesome growth in "real" production, because this year's computers are so tremendously valuable in terms of last year's theoretical prices.

So what effect does this scenario have on the statistics? For one thing, inflation will be understated, because the government averages a lot of huge price drops for computers that really only had small price drops. The other side of the coin is that growth will be overstated.... Therefore, real output growth, and anything derived from it, is overstated. Productivity appears to be growing quickly, and anything "real" in the national accounts—real GDP growth, real profit growth, real consumption growth, etc.—is actually less real than you might think.

Grant, through these experts and his own analysis, found serious flaws in the productivity miracle on which Greenspan seemed to base his decisions—and nearly all of his speeches. It follows logically that if the premise on which he based his conclusions was badly flawed, then so were the conclusions. By extension, Greenspan's decisions affecting the economy were also likely to be flawed—and, as history has proved, they were.

The Chairman demonstrated just how disoriented he could be, when at the June 2000 FOMC meeting he said, "I think the evidence that the economy is slowing to a certain extent is pretty much unambiguous.... In any event, I think the evidence of an actual recession at this point is belied by the fact that there is no evidence of which I am aware that suggests any deterioration in productivity growth."

In essence, Greenspan suggested that the U.S. economy couldn't be heading into a recession because he could see no slowing in productivity growth, all of which made for a very creative theory. But, even if Greenspan's thesis was correct, which it wasn't, he was working with flawed data and hence was likely to arrive at an incorrect conclusion, especially since his other source for optimism—the projections of security analysts[2]—was nothing if not dubious:

> Long-term expectations of the security analysts, which we presume reflect the views of corporate management, have not diminished. Indeed, they continue to move up for both the high-tech and the old economy firms. [Author's note: Does he really believe in two economies—one old, one new?] Actually, there has been a slight downtick in long-term

expectations of high-tech firms, but it is very small considering the fact that the stock prices for the sector have come down so markedly. Presumably, the market decline did damp some views of future earnings, but there's little evidence of that in the data.

What is remarkable is that Greenspan placed as much faith as he did in security analysts' predictions when he knew that they were not the most objective and clear-thinking sources available. He as much as said so in the FOMC meeting on October 5, 1999:

> I'm not saying these [analysts'] forecasts are any good as far as their earnings projections are concerned. Indeed, they're awful. They are biased on the upside, as they are made by people who are getting paid largely to project rising earnings to sell stocks, which is the business of the people who employ them.

Nevertheless, the Chairman continued to remain upbeat as the year wore on. At the FOMC meeting on August 22, 2000, he observed that capital investment continued to boom, and that was an indication that the expected rates of return, which he had previously determined to be on the rise, actually had materialized. Also at this meeting, Greenspan cited once again his arguably flawed secondary source for optimism, though he does take a step back from his prior faith in the predictions of security analysts: "We are seeing increasing long-term earnings forecasts by security analysts. As I have mentioned before, the latter may not be very knowledgeable about what is going on in the business world, but they are reasonably good reporters of what the companies they follow are saying about their longer-term outlooks." It is arguable whether or not security analysts are even the good reporters Greenspan claimed they were. My experience in many cases suggests otherwise. However, even if they were "good reporters," as Greenspan suggested, there is no guarantee that corporate management can accurately assess the future or, if it can, at what moment in time it shares the analysis with those analysts.

It's scary to think that the opinion of one group, whose opinion was based on that of another group, helped shape the economic opinion of the man who was in charge of picking the right interest rate to run a $10 trillion economy. But it may help explain some of his errors.

In any case, Greenspan's viewpoint remained constant throughout the fall of 2000. Whether at FOMC meetings or in speeches, he stuck with the same rhetoric that productivity growth was still on the upswing and, as we have seen, that seemed to be the holy grail as far as Greenspan was concerned. The stock market, however, was a different story. It appeared not to care what the Chairman thought about productivity growth. The May lows were breached in mid-November, and by the time the FOMC meeting on December 19, 2000, was called to order, the Nasdaq composite was about 38 percent lower for the year. It had collapsed 50 percent from its peak just nine months earlier, with approximately $2.5 trillion of market capitalization having been lost over that period.

One could easily argue that the March top was a false reference point—in other words, a place the market had no business being in the first place. Thus, the losses were somewhat ephemeral, as those gains never really existed. While there is truth in that observation, a lot of investors were badly hurt nonetheless.

At that December meeting, economic weakness was clearly on the minds of the committee members, as recession was mentioned 26 times before Greenspan launched into his own unique view of the economy. The committee members had good reason to talk about a recession, as the economy had peaked in the first quarter of 2000, along with the bubble. The Chairman, however, wasn't so sure: "The key question, and one that we cannot answer, is whether the growth has stabilized. At this point we cannot know…. The problem, as I've indicated on numerous occasions and as a number of you have commented, is that we do not have the capability of reliably forecasting a recession."

Numerous occasions?! First it was bubbles, and then it was recession. It seems that whenever the Chairman faced a truly important subject, he feigned ignorance.

The prior spring, at a Congressional hearing, he claimed he couldn't define *money*, the very thing the Fed regulated, saying that the difficulty came in defining the part of the liquidity structure that was truly money. He actually said that it wasn't "possible to manage something" you couldn't define. Since he was in charge of monetary policy for the country, he had all but admitted he was flying by the seat of his pants.

Returning to that December FOMC meeting, though Greenspan expressed concern that the high price of energy might spark a recession, he preferred not to cut rates. For a man who had cut rates indiscriminately over the course of his entire tenure, this reluctance was especially puzzling. If ever there was a perfect time to cut rates, this was it.

But Greenspan claimed he wasn't sure "confidence [had] been breached," and he didn't want to cut rates. He did, however, provide an anecdote illustrating what sort of psychological information he found unpersuasive:

> Very obviously stock market price declines, and clearly the Nasdaq declines, have a major impact on the investments in high-tech industries. I have gotten calls from a number of high-tech executives who are telling me that the market is dissolving rapidly before their eyes. But I suspect that a not inconceivable possibility is that what is dissolving before their eyes is their own personal net worth! (*Laughter*) That does bias one's view of what is happening

in the world. So, we have to be a little careful about being seduced by those types of evaluations.

True, he made committee members laugh when he observed "a not inconceivable possibility is that what is dissolving before their eyes is their own personal net worth." But he didn't elaborate on the types of *evaluations* he used to arrive at his own psychological determinations regarding his confidence concerning the economy or the stock market. His reluctance to cut rates at this meeting was even more perplexing given his admission that "it is quite conceivable that we may have to have a telephone conference and move the rate before the next meeting." The most likely explanation for this reluctance was that he was quite sanguine that the economy was just fine.

The Chairman summed up where he stood at the end of the meeting as he and FOMC committee members wrestled with the verbiage to use in the press release. Arguing for his point of view, he announced: "What we basically would be saying is that the economy is going down. We don't have that view." Funny, because that was precisely what the economy was doing.

Things were about to get worse. Although the stock market essentially drifted sideways into the end of the 2000, it broke to the downside at the start of the new year.

In the first two days of January 2001, the S&P 500 dropped almost 10 percent and the Nasdaq sank 12 percent. On January 3, 2001, the Chairman called an emergency FOMC meeting. He wanted to cut rates by half of a percentage point to 6 percent. What had happened in two weeks to precipitate this radical change of view? It wasn't economic data, as very little new information, with the exception of Christmas sales, was available in those two weeks.

At the emergency meeting, Greenspan seemed to point to what he saw as the growing concerns of the analysts to account for his own change of heart (though it seems unlikely that their views could have changed that much in those two weeks):

As you probably are all acutely aware, the S&P earnings per share numbers are being revised down at a fairly aggressive pace week-by-week, to the point that now the analysts' estimates for both the fourth quarter and the current first quarter are negative versus a year ago. To be sure, the analysts have revised their numbers upward for the second half of 2001 and 2002, but the problem here is the difficulty of getting a handle on what is clearly a decelerating path. And at this stage there is as yet no evidence that the downward revisions on the part of the analysts have come to an end. As we've all observed, orders are weakening across the board. Pockets of high-tech strength persist, but generally we're seeing a very poor orders pattern and deterioration in a number of the industrial sectors of the economy.

It is not clear what orders were "weakening across the board" on January 3, 2001, that weren't on December 19, 2000. Aside from the lackluster Christmas sales and an expectation of disappointing auto sales, Greenspan didn't explain where the shocking weakness was emanating from. Nonetheless, transcripts from that early January meeting document Greenspan as saying that "in our estimates, we're reducing the real GDP growth by 1½ percentage points for the first quarter, leaving it at 1.7 percent." He actually sounded a bit scared: "As I said previously, however, we're certainly not yet in a free fall. I say 'not yet' because a free fall doesn't look like a free fall until you really start falling."

In reality, the only thing that had collapsed in those two weeks was stock prices, and that had just occurred in the two days prior to the emergency meeting. Greenspan seemed panicked by the new year's falling stock market and apparently used the analysts' comments and weak order data as his cover story. But, to ensure that all his bases were covered, the Chairman made a stab at a potential scapegoat, saying that "an inventory readjustment process" was underway. He qualified that observation a bit. "To be sure, inventory–sales ratios have not been going up in any general way, but they have flattened out after being on a pronounced long-term downward trend." He didn't sound too convinced.

Nonetheless Greenspan *was* convinced about one thing; he was determined not to cast any aspersions on his pet theory of technology-generated productivity growth: "Actually, one thing that I think is important is to indicate in our press statement that there is little evidence to date of any deterioration in the long-term advances in technology and the related expansion in productivity."

The truth was that the economy *was* under pressure as a result of the bursting stock market bubble. Greenspan obviously didn't understand that, which was why he hadn't eased rates at the December 19, 2000, FOMC meeting. But something had definitely spooked him, and the stock market decline is the likely culprit. As he observed during the Fed's emergency January meeting: "It's the change in tone and the speed with which it seems to be occurring that is terrible and that this move could help." The break apparently had him worried, so he was going to cut rates and catch investors by surprise.

The fact that Greenspan refused to cut rates at the regularly scheduled FOMC meeting on December 19, 2000, but did so at the emergency meeting on January 3, 2001, is a subtle yet enormous difference. This move demonstrated that Greenspan did not have a handle on what was happening with the economy but was pushed into action when the stock market experienced a couple of bad days. However, it was by surprising the stock market that he reinforced for all the world to see the notion of the Greenspan Put. This fomented more speculation—which is exactly what had caused so much carnage to begin with.

When Greenspan surprised the market on January 3, 2001, with a half percentage point reduction in rates down to 6 percent, the response was explosive. In just five minutes, S&P 500 index futures rocketed 5 percent, just as they had done when he surprised the market in October 1998.

By the time the day was over, the Nasdaq had jumped 14 percent—the largest one-day advance in the stock market's history. The Chairman had reignited speculation once again. It wouldn't last, however, as the now deflated stock bubble had created an enormous undertow.

On February 13, 2001, the Chairman gave a speech, which that day I dubbed "An Ode to Productivity," that further proves he had no idea what was unfolding in the economy or the stock market. The reason again was that he never understood that *he* had precipitated a massive stock market bubble. As a result, Greenspan couldn't grasp its dramatic consequences.

Moreover, although recent short-term business profits have softened considerably, most corporate *man-*

*agers appear not to have altered to any appreciable
extent their long-standing optimism about the future
returns from using new technology.* [italics mine] A
recent survey of purchasing managers suggests that
the wave of new online business-to-business activities
is far from cresting. Corporate managers more generally, rightly or wrongly, appear to remain remarkably sanguine about the potential for innovations to
continue to enhance productivity and profits. At least
this is what is gleaned from the projections of equity
analysts, who, one must presume, obtain most of
their insights from corporate managers. According to
one prominent survey, the three- to five-year average
earnings projections of more than a thousand analysts, though exhibiting some signs of diminishing in
recent months, have generally held firm at a very
high level.

In other words, even though we had experienced a bit
of short-term weakness, technology and productivity
were still going to take us to the Promised Land. Of this,
Greenspan was sure—because Wall Street analysts, those
bastions of independent and accurate thinking, were still
optimistic.

He went on to exclaim: "Expected earnings growth
over the longer-run continues to be elevated. If the forces
contributing to long-term productivity growth remain
intact, the degree of retrenchment will presumably be

limited. Prospects for high productivity growth should, with time, bolster both consumption and investment demand. Before long in this scenario, excess inventories would be run off to desired levels."

As with most fairy tales, this one had the perfect ending. Productivity growth would drive demand and the *modest* inventory correction the economy was experiencing would soon end. Greenspan's love affair with productivity growth allowed him to rationalize the bubble in the first place, and now it prevented him from understanding why there had been one, which rendered him incapable of discerning just what was wrong with the economy.

What is even more remarkable is that the collapse in the stock market even met his own limited definition of a bubble, which he had stated nearly two years before in front of Congress:

> The question I was asking, abstractly [in 1996], [was] how will we know when markets are gripped by "irrational exuberance," and I didn't have the answer on that particular point. I think I have an answer now— one that is very difficult to judge, except in retrospect. If any stock market ... falls by 30 or 40 percent in a matter of weeks or a very few months, I will grant that there was a bubble back there.

Apparently, believing in the miracles of productivity growth meant never having to say "there was a bubble," even if what transpired met his very definition of the phenomenon. Unfortunately, his confidence in the miracles of productivity was misplaced.

Since productivity growth was the holy grail of Greenspan's beliefs, it is worth taking the time to understand just how flawed the data was with which he was working. Just two days after the Chairman's productivity speech, James Grant published a follow-up article to his 2000 exposé on the subject of the inherent optimistic bias of hedonic adjustments, which were applied to the data Greenspan was championing. Grant's article eviscerated the concept of escalating productivity growth.

As Grant explained in the article, hedonic adjustments were meant to capture improvements in products' quality and adjust their price changes accordingly, as was discussed in Chapter 2. In the case of computers, for instance, hedonics would try to capture improvements in processor speed or disk drive capacity and amend their prices in view of such "improvements." In the fourth quarter of 2000, the country spent $118.2 billion (annualized) on computers and peripherals. But, as Grant explained, after those improvements were captured by government statisticians at the Commerce Department, the "real" amount of investment (the measure used in productivity calculations) in computers and peripherals became $329 billion annualized. Thus, the "real" dollars spent were 2.8 times greater than the nominal dollars (the kind one uses at the grocery store). The difference, as it was slightly larger than 2 percent of GDP (or roughly $210.8 billion), was a nontrivial number. In fact, these purely statistical, nonexistent dollars made up roughly 25 percent of GDP growth that quarter. In his article, Grant quoted noted late economist and newsletter founder Dr. Kurt Richebacher, who made the astute observation that this statistically created "production" was "nobody's expenses, and also nobody's revenues."

But this wasn't just a problem for the fourth quarter of 2000—these calculations had been distorting the data for *many years*. According to a paper by Lynne E. Browne, director of research at the Boston Fed, "while nominal investments in computers and peripherals rose roughly 10 percent per year between 1995 and 1999, real investment [the statistically enhanced version] rose 45 percent a year."

Grant's article explained why understanding the difference between nominal investments and real investments in technology mattered: "The value produced by these [hedonic] adjustments *echoes throughout the national income accounts.* [italics mine] They have contributed to faster measured growth in GDP. And because productivity is defined as output divided by hours worked, a higher level of output yields a faster rate of productivity growth than would otherwise be obtained."

Thus, if output was overstated due to erroneous statistical enhancement, then productivity growth was overstated as well! Furthermore, even though productivity growth during the late 1990s was boosted by hedonics, as Figure 6 makes clear, the period still was nothing extraordinary by historic standards.

In sum, although the U.S. economy did experience respectable productivity growth in the late 1990s, the productivity miracle that Greenspan was talking about was a statistical mirage that led him to repeatedly come to incorrect conclusions. As an aside to this discussion,

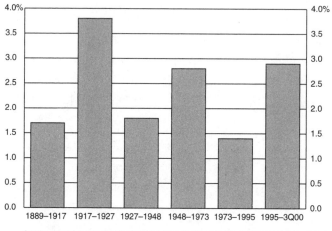

Grant's Interest Rate Observer, Pre-1948 data from John Kendrick, "Productivity Trends in the United States," published for the National Bureau of Economic Research; remainder from U.S. Bureau of Labor Statistics

Figure 6 Productivity Growth — The Long View

it's worth mentioning that the Commerce Department quietly dropped the use of hedonic adjustments for computers in 2003.

Greenspan had cut rates one-half of 1 percent in January 2000—just two weeks before his now infamous productivity speech—and he would continue to cut rates *at every meeting that entire year*. That's not all; Greenspan made three surprise rate cuts outside of the scheduled meetings, for a grand total of *eleven rate cuts for 2001*.

By year end, the Fed funds rate would stand at just 1.75 percent, a whopping 76 percent lower than the 6.5 percent it fetched when the year began. As significant as those cuts were, they were overshadowed by the unwinding bubble. The stock market continued to drop steadily throughout the winter, spring, and summer. By September 10, 2001, the Nasdaq had declined roughly 34 percent for the year, while the S&P 500 index had sunk 18 percent.

Obviously something was very wrong, and Greenspan's furious rate cutting had no effect on the stock market, though those rate cuts probably kept the economy from deteriorating further than it did.

Chapter 6

Home Sweet Home: Housing Saves Us from the Stock Bubble
(2001–2003)

With the "New Economy" discredited along with the technology bust, Greenspan now embraces housing as the new miracle economic driver. Real estate booms thanks to rates as low as 1 percent, the magic of financial "innovation," adjustable-rate mortgages, and the "use your house as ATM" mentality. An even more dangerous bubble is born.

The terrible tragedy of September 11, 2001, was not the primary reason for the declining stock market or the weak economy in late 2001 and 2002, though both were obviously negatively impacted by the terrorist attacks on the United States and the disruptions that followed. While that distinction may appear unimportant, it's significant because 9/11 made many people forget about the financial free fall we were already in. After that day, almost all economic and financial problems were blamed on its events. September 11 exacerbated problems that were already in existence, but it was not the root cause.

When the stock market reopened for trading on September 17, 2001, part of my column that day focused on the preexisting nature of the country's financial problems. I felt it was especially important for people to understand the true origin of those problems just as they tried to grasp the ramifications of the recent attack:

> The fact that the stock market and the economy are under pressure is a function of the bubble that was permitted to go on for so long in the late 1990s. Once we experienced a bubble of this enormous dimension, it was preordained that there would be future economic and financial market dislocations. Contrary to what the media has been saying, the terrorist action only served to exacerbate trends already well underway. People were already re-examining

their reasons for owning stocks at the prevailing prices. Slowly, they were coming to the conclusion that the stock market might be riskier than they thought. The stock market has been under pressure since it peaked in March 2000. Alan Greenspan's halo has been slipping for some time as it has become increasingly clear that he does not control the economy. The exogenous event that we just witnessed will accelerate that process and produce socioeconomic ramifications that will become clearer as time goes by. To repeat, the stock market and economic pressures are not a direct result of last week's terrorist action. The latter was an accelerant to trends that were already well established.

A few days later the *Wall Street Journal* ran a story by Steve Liesman headlined "Profits Downturn Could Be the Worst Since the Late 1960s." The lead sentence read, "The economic fallout from last week's terrorist attack could *extend* the current corporate profits recession into one of the longest and deepest of at least the past 34 years." Sir John Templeton, too, saw the preexisting nature of the problems. In early October 2001, he weighed in on the size of the bubble in an interview that appeared on the MSN Web site, explaining that "the greatest financial insanity to ever enter any nation was what happened with the technology stocks up until 18 months ago." The country's financial troubles were due to the stock market bubble that had burst. But as time wore on, the bubble was swept aside as the culprit, while the country focused on recovering from 9/11.

At the handful of FOMC meetings that took place in the final months of 2001, Greenspan spent little time discussing technology or productivity. At the meeting on November 6, 2001, he sounded worried and he was certainly confused: "We keep forecasting stabilization but there has been no evidence of it anywhere.... We currently are observing the obverse of the extraordinary accelerations that occurred in world economies during the latter part of the 1990s as a consequence of increased globalization—a development now seen as a two-edged sword." The Chairman had apparently now decided that it was *globalization* that created the former glory years of the late 1990s, not technology and productivity as had been repeatedly claimed in the past, and we in America were now experiencing the downside of that trend.

The FOMC meeting on December 11, 2001, was the last one for that year and the last one for which transcripts were available when this book was written in late 2007. In an interesting portend of the next bubble to come, it was noteworthy in that the word *mortgage* was mentioned 40 times. In addition, an important feature of that upcoming bubble was already on the Chairman's radar screen: "we are seeing this very high sensitivity to long-term mortgage rates, for example in the extraction of home equity that tends to lead promptly to consumption expenditures." Just as noteworthy, in a moment of unusual insight for the FOMC, district Fed president Michael Moskow, while voicing his concern over the economy, acknowledged the elephant in the room, stating: "I think we may have a good deal further to go in unwinding the capital overhang that became evident following the bursting of the high-tech bubble."

As had become customary with bubble-oriented comments, it was completely ignored by the committee.

As 2002 began, the real estate bubble was still a ways off. Meanwhile, there was plenty of damage from the stock bubble yet to be endured. In the year 2002, the Nasdaq would decline another 32 percent, while the S&P 500 would sink 24 percent (see Figure 7 on page 138). From its peak in 2000, the Nasdaq would fall a stunning 74 percent, the S&P 500 by a not insubstantial 43 percent.

On February 27, 2002, Greenspan appeared before the House Financial Services Committee. This testimony began his first serious effort toward revising the history of what had transpired in the previous three years. In discussing the economic problems, he focused on the falloff in demand that occurred due to the overcapacity that had developed. He failed to utter one word about the bubble which had caused the overcapacity to begin with. This misallocation of capital that occurred as a result of money chasing technology ideas, like telecommunication companies and dot-com "businesses," was what created the overcapacity. This was where the "capital overhang" came from that Moskow noted at the prior FOMC meeting.

To the committee, Greenspan trotted out his fallback excuse, making the case that were it not for 9/11, the recession that began in 2000 might have ended already: "However, before the terrorist attacks, it was far from obvious that this concurrent weakness was becoming self-enforcing. Indeed, immediately prior to September 11, some sectors exhibited tentative signs of stabilization contributing to a hope that the worst of the previous cumulative weakness in world economic activity was nearing an end." Obviously, neither case can be proved because 9/11 *did* happen, but given the weakness in stocks and the economy during 2001, it was a huge stretch to suggest that the economy was poised to recover. Next he discussed what he believed to be an important cause of the economic weakness at that time:

> The retrenchment in capital spending over the past year and a half was central to the sharp slowing we experienced in overall activity. The steep rise in high-tech spending that occurred in the post-Y2K months was clearly not sustainable. The demand for many of the newer technologies was growing rapidly, but capacity was expanding even faster.

In actuality, it was the spending both before and after Y2K that was unsustainable. Nevertheless, that fact was one which Greenspan either didn't see or didn't understand. He then made an assertion that flew in the face of all the evidence: as a result of this unsustainable capital spending "businesses require that new investments pay off much more rapidly than they had previously." In other words, the country hadn't experienced a slowdown exacerbated by a bubble-induced mountain of overcapacity. He apparently wanted us to believe that corporate spending was weaker because corporations had shortened their required payback period.

Finally, Greenspan had a point he wanted everyone to be aware of, that this particular downturn was "significantly milder...than the long history of business cycles would lead us to expect." The reasons for that, in summary, were technology—"real-time information has played a key role"—and financial innovation. "New financial products—including derivatives, asset-backed securities, collateralized loan obligations, and collateralized mortgage obligations.... Lenders have the opportunity to be considerably more diversified, and borrowers are far less dependent on specific institutions for funds.... They have contributed to the development of a far more flexible and efficient financial system."

I don't want to get ahead of myself, but do any of these terms sound familiar? Asset-backed securities, collateralized mortgage obligations, collateralized loans ... these are the very same instruments that led to the financial market turmoil of late 2007 in which so many huge financial firms were crippled. It was typical Greenspan: extolling the virtues of ideas he didn't fully comprehend that he felt would take us to the Promised Land. They led to tears instead.

Greenspan was right when he said that the recession was not as severe as "the long history of business cycles would suggest." But given that by mid-2003 he would have slashed interest rates by another three-quarters of 1 percent, to the microscopic level of 1 percent, it's unlikely he had much confidence in his observation.

In reality, the economy was not saved by technology or financial innovation. However, the true savior can be found within his testimony. As the seeds of the next disaster were being sown in the form of home mortgage extraction, the Chairman extolled the benefits:

> Moreover, attractive mortgage rates have bolstered the sales of existing homes and the extraction of capital gains embedded in home equity that those sales engender. Low rates have also encouraged households to take on larger mortgages when refinancing their homes. Drawing on home equity in this manner is a significant source of funding for consumption and home modernization.

Though it was very slow in developing speed, the upcoming housing bubble would be the engine to lift the economy and stock market off the canvas—and the elixir that would wash away the bad memories created by the prior stock market implosion. Despite the ongoing corporate restructurings, write-offs, layoffs, scandals, and carnage in stock prices, housing activity was percolating along beneath the surface.

The housing market was not an object of speculation during most of the 1990s. From 1991 through 1995, the growth of total mortgage debt outstanding averaged just 3.7 percent. That growth rate accelerated, with the help of the equity bubble, to average 6.2 percent for 1996 and 1997. By 1998, it was galloping ahead at an annual rate of 9.5 percent. Around that time, housing prices began to accelerate as a result of the wealth produced by runaway stock prices. Stock prices were responsible for driving the real estate market higher thanks to the proliferation of stock option grants, by which so many people were allocated meaningful quantities of shares. This newfound wealth was used to buy nicer and bigger homes.

By the end of 2000, total mortgage debt outstanding stood at approximately $6.8 trillion, 50 percent higher than it had been at the end of 1995. And that $2.3 trillion increase had not gone unnoticed. Wall Street had been busy building up the infrastructure to securitize that mortgage debt (and would keep building it). In concert, government-sponsored enterprises such as Fannie

Mae and Freddie Mac were also expanding their activities at an aggressive pace. So, as Greenspan drove interest rates down from 6.5 percent in mid-2000 to 1.75 percent at the end of 2001, he was pouring water on ground that was already quite fertile.

In the recession year of 2001, the country didn't just refinance mortgage debt, *it took on 10.2 percent more.* Lower rates made it possible for homeowners to assume more debt. That extra debt could be used to purchase a more expensive house or extract equity to pay bills, buy a new car, or purchase some other toy. As the volume of mortgage debt grew, Wall Street and the mortgage industry *innovated* to use the Chairman's term. The public also innovated as it became comfortable with the process and house prices continued to rise. In the year 2002, outstanding mortgage debt grew by 11.7 percent. It increased by $1.57 trillion in 2001 and 2002 combined, an increase that was over 15 percent of GDP (which expanded by just 6.6 percent over the same period). Though the stock market was delivering red ink, the real estate market was not.

In fact, the real estate market had been hot enough that at an appearance before Congress on April 17, 2002, Greenspan felt it necessary to make a statement: "The ongoing strength in the housing market has raised concerns about the possible emergence of a bubble in home prices." The country was gripped in an ongoing bear market for stocks, yet the action in the real estate market was wild enough to be a focus of the Chairman's testimony. Greenspan then proceeded to explain why in his opinion real estate was "especially ill suited to develop into a bubble":

> The analogy often made to the building and bursting of a stock price bubble is imperfect. First, unlike in the stock market, sales in the real estate market incur substantial transactions costs and, when most homes are sold, the seller must physically move out.... Thus, while stock market turnover is more than 100 percent annually, the turnover of home ownership is less than 10 percent annually—scarcely tinder for speculative conflagration. Second, arbitrage opportunities are much more limited in housing markets than in securities markets. A home in Portland, Oregon, is not a close substitute for a home in Portland, Maine, and the "national" housing market is better understood as a collection of small, local housing markets. Even if a bubble were to develop in a local market, it would not necessarily have implications for the nation as a whole.

Obviously, none of his three arguments prevented the United States from experiencing the housing bubble that burst in 2007. They were superficial at best and unlikely to deter speculators one iota. As usual, Greenspan did leave himself an out: "These factors certainly do not mean that bubbles cannot develop in house markets and that home prices cannot decline: Indeed, home prices fell significantly in several parts of the country in the early 1990s." That said, it was clear where he stood: he didn't believe in the concept of a housing bubble "because the turnover of homes is so much smaller than that of stocks and because the underlying demand for living space tends to be revised very gradually, the speed and magnitude of price rises and declines often observed in markets for securities are more difficult to create in markets for homes." If his view was correct, then how did Japan experience such a massive real estate bubble in the 1980s? One can only imagine what Greenspan's answer to that question might have been. That particular bubble was followed by an excruciating wipeout that lasted over a decade; real estate prices declined over 90 percent.

By the summer of 2002, wild stories of real estate speculation in the United States, though ones that would sound tame compared to those that came later, were commonplace. On August 20, 2002, the *Wall Street Journal* carried a story headlined "C'mon, My House Is Worth More Than That," which chronicled the extent to which people were now pressuring their appraisers to maximize the amount of money they could borrow against the value of their homes. According to the article, one appraiser said a prospective client warned, "If you're not going to come up with the number I want, I'm not going to pay you."

Such threats were becoming increasingly more common, as people's sense of entitlement grew along with their greed. That fact comes across loud and clear in another quote from that article, this one by an appraiser from Des Moines, Iowa, who received a call from an unhappy homeowner: "With my appraisal, the bank wouldn't give him sufficient money to buy the boat he wanted. I said, 'Buy a smaller boat.' He didn't like that answer." While this fellow didn't get his way, he was an exception. Folks everywhere were pushing the envelope and being rewarded for doing so. It was as if the public—and Wall Street, for that matter—had learned nothing from the losses inflicted by the bear market they had just endured. On August 30, 2002, Greenspan gave a speech at the Kansas City Fed's annual boondoggle, which is held in Jackson Hole, Wyoming. In this speech, the Maestro maneuvered to rewrite the history of the stock market bubble (which, mind you, was still unwinding at the time) in an effort to absolve himself and the Fed of any bubble-related blame. Greenspan made many unsupportable statements during his career, but this speech in particular deserves some special attention. He would continue to use a variation of it repeatedly for the remainder of his years at the Fed.

Greenspan began in defense mode, stating what a difficult position the stock market bubble placed him in: "We were confronted with forces that none of us had personally experienced. Aside from the then-recent experience of Japan, only history books and musty archives gave us clues to the appropriate stance for policy."

The Japanese twin bubbles of stocks and real estate had only burst in 1989—just over a decade prior. It was a perfect example of what *not* to do, that is, wait too long to address the market imbalances. Meanwhile, it was simultaneously also a perfect reminder of the lesson that history books teach us over and over again: bubbles—and the enormous misallocation of capital that goes with them—should be avoided at all costs.

The Chairman then argued that bubbles were so powerful that they didn't respond to rate hikes: "From mid-1999 through May 2000, the federal funds rate was raised 150 basis points. However, equity price increases were largely undeterred during that period despite what now, in retrospect, was the exhausted tail of a bull market."

Given what we have learned regarding Greenspan's role in fomenting the bubble, the lameness of this excuse requires no rebuttal, but it is worth pointing out that he describes the end of the bubble as "the exhausted tail of a bull market." He *still* can't admit it was a bubble, even as he defends himself against his culpability for the bubble. His excuses continued: "The notion that a well-timed incremental tightening could have been calibrated to prevent the late 1990s' bubble is almost surely an illusion." Here at least Greenspan is correct. A small, surgical, incremental, painless tightening would have done little, but that is the wrong yardstick in the first place. However, his implication that it's an illusion to think you can prevent a bubble is false.

The final excuse Greenspan trotted out that day was perhaps the most galling: "It seems reasonable to generalize from our recent experience that no low-risk, low-cost, incremental monetary tightening exists that can reliably deflate a bubble. But is there some policy that can at least limit the size of a bubble and, hence, its destructive fallout? From the evidence to date, the answer appears to be no."

Though he did note "the destructive fallout" that occurred in the aftermath of the bubble bursting, he seems to have forgotten what he said at the FOMC meeting on September 24, 1996, but I haven't:

> We do have the possibility of raising major concerns by increasing margin requirements. I guarantee that if you want to get rid of the bubble, whatever it is, that will do it. My concern is that I'm not sure what else it will do.

He knew that raising margin requirements would send a powerful signal, but he didn't take that action because he didn't believe that what was transpiring in the market was a bubble. So now, in 2002, Greenspan shifted to the excuse that *nothing can stop a bubble*. He argued that, in essence, he was powerless to stop it, even if he *had* recognized it in the first place. Therefore, of course, he was not to blame.

Greenspan may have anticipated this line of questioning, and so, in a footnote to his speech, he tried to deflect it: "Some have asserted that the Federal Reserve can deflate a stock-price bubble—rather painlessly—by boosting margin requirements. The evidence [Author's note: which, it should be added, he doesn't cite] suggests otherwise."

On the contrary, his own opinion, as we saw, and the practices of various futures exchanges suggest that such action by the Fed would have worked well. As for his footnote, it's almost a non sequitur; I can't imagine anyone would claim that behavior modification, which would be one goal of raising margin requirements, would be "rather painless." Nor should it be.

Greenspan labored quite hard to make the case that he was blameless. And for the most part, he got away with it (at least he did back then). Remarkably little criticism came his way. He must have felt like a guy who had just won the lottery. *The Economist*, however, wasn't buying his story. In a September 7, 2002, article titled "To Burst or Not to Burst?" the magazine pointed out the error in his logic:

> The correct test is not whether a bubble can be deflated without some loss of output. Rather, it is whether the early pricing of a bubble causes less pain than letting it grow only to burst later. The longer a bubble is allowed to inflate, the more it encourages the build-up of other imbalances, such as too much borrowing and investment, which have the power to turn a mild downturn into something nastier.

An editorial was published in the same issue that zeroed in on another aspect of the Chairman's behavior during the bubble as well as its ramifications:

> A less forgivable mistake was that Mr. Greenspan acted as something of a cheerleader for the "new economy." Even if some of the increase in productivity growth was real, his enthusiasm contributed to investors' euphoria. They seized on all of his comments to justify their bullishness about future profits. Ironically, Mr. Greenspan was among the first to give warning of a bubble in 1996, drawing attention to the market's "irrational exuberance." What a pity he failed to put America's monetary policy where his mouth (briefly) was.

The Economist's sound rationale for working diligently to prevent a bubble is worth remembering as we begin to explore the buildup of the real estate bubble, which will ultimately dwarf the previous equity bubble and pose far greater risks to the country and the world.

In October 2002, even as stock prices were hitting their lows for the bear market after having declined for almost three years, the real estate market was sporting multi-year gains. Between the autumns of 1997 and 2002, the

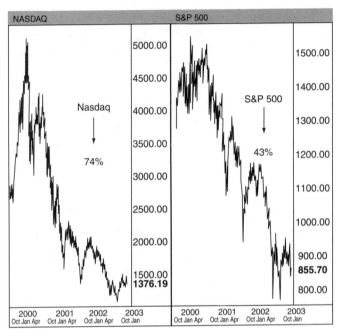

Molly Evans

Figure 7 Was the Climb Worth the Fall?

average house price in the United States rose 42 percent. In New York City, the prices had risen 67 percent; in Jersey City, 75 percent; in Boston, 69 percent; and in San Francisco, 88 percent.[1] Real estate was becoming the new object of desire and wealth (much like the Dutch tulip bulb craze discussed in Chapter 2). Many households had turned themselves into quasi-hedge funds. As interest rates fell, homeowners refinanced their houses and increased their leverage by cashing out the principal they had previously paid down. (In the early 1980s, homeowners' average equity equaled 70 percent of the house's market value; by 2003, it was down to only 55 percent.)

A clear early indication of the use-your-home-as-an-ATM strategy was a November 2002 *Time* magazine article, which offered up-to-the-minute advice: 'Borrow against your house to buy stocks now.'

In his testimony before Congress on November 13, 2002, Greenspan explained how the nascent real estate bubble had helped bail out the deflating equity bubble, at least as far as the economy was concerned:

> Besides sustaining the demand for new construction, mortgage markets have also been a powerful stabilizing force over the past two years of economic distress by facilitating the extraction of some of the equity that homeowners had built up over the years.

Greenspan also explained how the process had worked to save the day:

> These data and some preliminary econometric results suggest that a dollar of equity extracted from housing has a more powerful effect on consumer spending than does a dollar change in the value of common stocks. Of course, the net decline in the market value of stocks has greatly exceeded the

additions to capital gains on homes over the past two years. So, despite the greater apparent sensitivity of consumption to capital gains on homes, the net effect of all changes in household wealth on consumer spending since early 2000 has been negative.... That said, it is important to recognize that the extraction of equity from homes has been a significant support to consumption during a period when other asset prices were declining sharply. Were it not for this phenomenon, economic activity would have been notably weaker in the wake of the decline in the value of household financial assets.

In other words, productivity was out; housing was the *new, new* miracle economic driver. As the budding housing bubble built steam, it helped both the economy and the stock market to slowly recover, which in turn helped reinforce the housing market, which then helped the economy and the stock market. And so it went. But so powerful was the undertow from the receding stock bubble that it ultimately took 13 interest rate cuts (to as low as 1 percent) and three major tax cuts to align the stars in such a way that a recovery could take place. It also took time. It wasn't until spring 2003 that the stock market began to recover and the economy finally began to march ahead with a bit of authority. (The massive monetary and fiscal policy stimulus required to produce that economic recovery should be kept in mind as we explore the housing bubble in future pages. This housing bubble will also be followed by a bust, but generating the next economic rebound will be even more difficult.)

The Fed would be exceedingly slow, once again, to reverse the rate slashing it had undertaken to fight the stock market bust. It found a new bad guy with which to rationalize its emergency low rates, and the enemy's name was *deflation*. That straw man had been set up the prior fall by then future Fed Chairman Ben Bernanke. On November 21, 2002, in a seminal speech titled "Deflation: Making Sure 'It' Doesn't Happen Here," Bernanke made his case as to why it wouldn't.

> Like gold, U.S. dollars have value only to the extent that they are strictly limited in supply. But the U.S. government has a technology, called a printing press (or, today, its electronic equivalent), that allows it to produce as many U.S. dollars as it wishes at essentially no cost. By increasing the number of U.S. dollars in circulation, or even by credibly threatening to do so, the U.S. government can also reduce the value of a dollar in terms of goods and services, which is equivalent to raising the prices in dollars of those goods and services. We

conclude that, under a paper-money system, a determined government can always generate higher spending and hence positive inflation.

Due to the nature of politicians, who tend to promise more than they can deliver in a social democracy such as the United States, it is not deflation that presents a problem. The reality is that governments will cheat their citizens over time via *in*flation. But there's no telling in advance at what rate they will do so. People seem to confuse declining asset markets with "deflation." To clarify, deflation means that the value of the dollar appreciates against a basket of goods and services. Or said differently, it means that a dollar will buy more for you in the future than it does today. That outcome was not in danger of occurring in 2003 (or at any other time since Nixon closed the gold window in 1970).

In light of the Chairman and the future Chairman's angst over deflation, it might be useful to take a moment and review what has happened to the purchasing power of the dollar over time. Figure 8 illustrates this phenomenon via a product that we can all appreciate — a Hershey's chocolate bar.

No doubt you've noticed that occasionally either the price of a Hershey's bar goes up or the size of the bar shrinks. Figure 8 depicts the fluctuations in the price of an ounce of chocolate, in a Hershey's chocolate bar, from 1908 to the present. What you can see is that — surprise,

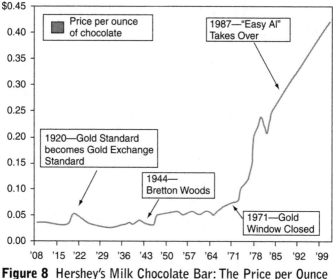

Figure 8 Hershey's Milk Chocolate Bar: The Price per Ounce

surprise!—the cost of chocolate per ounce has risen over time and in fact has increased more than twelvefold. Measured in this way, the dollar has lost 92 percent of its purchasing power since 1908. That, as illustrated by a simple chocolate bar, is what inflation does over time.

Just before the Fed made its thirteenth and final (for that cycle) interest rate cut on June 25, 2003, Jeff Opdyke and Michelle Higgins published a timely article that appeared in the *Wall Street Journal* titled "What Deflation? Why Your Bills Are Rising." The piece delivered a succinct description of what all of us who live in the real world already knew:

> If the Federal Reserve is so concerned about deflation, why are so many of the everyday costs of life on the rise? Postage stamps, sporting events, auto insurance, real estate taxes and even haircuts have been increasing in price in recent years at a faster pace than the official inflation rate.
>
> The government's consumer price index has increased an average of just 2.5 percent annually over the past three years. In the same period, by some measures, cable TV costs are up 9.1 percent annually, auto insurance is up 7.6 percent a year, and even movie popcorn is up more than 3 percent. Health care costs, college tuition and the price of heating your home have been rising at far faster rates—in the case of natural gas, around 21.4 percent a year.

What Greenspan, Bernanke, and the Fed were worried about was at odds with what Americans were experiencing on a daily basis. Or, as Richard Yamarone, the chief economist of Argus Research, was quoted in this article, "no matter where you go, no matter who you talk to, prices are on the rise."

There was no real chance of deflation actually occurring because, as Bernanke said, the Fed had a printing press at its disposal. But the Fed and Greenspan's preoccupation with deflation gave them the cover story to drive rates lower than they needed to be and to hold them there far longer than they should have. The final blow was dealt on June 25, 2003, when the Chairman cut rates for the *thirteenth* time. This final cut of one-quarter of 1 percent took rates to 1 percent, where Greenspan would keep them for *nearly a year*. The effect of those too-low rates was felt most directly in the real estate market, but they also penalized anyone who saved money and tried to live off of the interest those savings generated.

By July 2003, the real estate market had become frothy enough to garner more of the public's attention. That year in his annual interview with Robert J. Flaherty of *Equities* magazine, Sir John Templeton, one of the world's most optimistic and successful investors, noted how unusual the relationship was between stocks and real estate: "Every previous major bear market has been accompanied by a bear market in home prices.... This time, home prices have gone up 20 percent, and this represents a very dangerous situation." He then explained what would eventually happen to home prices, though I'm sure he didn't expect that it wouldn't occur some five years into the future: "When home prices do start [to go] down, they will fall remarkably far. In Japan, home prices are down to less than half what they were at the stock market peak.... A home-price decline of as little as 20 percent would put a lot of people in bankruptcy."

He also warned about debt, a subject that we will explore in Chapter 7, saying:

Emphasize in your magazine how big the debt is.… The total debt of America is now $31 trillion. That is three times the GNP of the U.S. That is unprecedented in a major nation. No nation has ever had such a big debt as America has, and it's bigger than it was at the peak of the stock market boom. Think of the dangers involved. Almost everyone has a home mortgage, and some are 89 percent of the value of the home. [Author's note: By 2007, many would be over 100 percent.] If home prices start down, there will be bankruptcies, and in bankruptcy, houses are sold at lower prices, pushing home prices down further.

The purpose of sharing Templeton's observations is to emphasize two key points:

1. In July 2003, there were already reasons to be concerned about real estate speculation and prices—though what transpired then was child's play relative to what took place over the course of the next four years.
2. You should remember Templeton's warning as you continue reading, since the real estate market grows far wilder than it was in 2003. Keep in

mind, too, that the risks Templeton anticipated escalated dramatically.

However wild one thought the real estate market was, it clearly wasn't unruly enough for members of the Fed to pay attention to it. They were still giving speeches about fighting deflation. About the same time that the Templeton interview was published, the Dallas Fed published a paper titled "Monetary Policy in a Zero-Interest-Rate Economy." Apparently, the Fed was so worried about deflation that it wanted to show that it had a plan to put into practice policies to create inflation, even if slashing interest rates to zero wasn't sufficient to do so.

The paper discussed, among other things, the possibility of the Fed buying real goods and services, or perhaps even other domestic securities—like longer-term Treasuries—but the most staggering idea it contemplated was taxing your savings. The paper's authors, Evan Koenig and Jim Dolmas, proposed the idea of a "stamp fee" or "carry tax," whereby a currency would have to be stamped periodically, and you would be charged for your currency "in order to retain its status as legal tender. The stamp fee could be calibrated to generate any negative, nominal interest rate the central bank desired." They toss out a few potential numbers, like, 1 percent a month, to validate your currency. In other words, it would *cost* you 12 percent a year to have the gall to save money.

Greenspan and the Fed were so out of touch with reality that they were worried about a fight to the death with deflation, as the real estate bubble was already gathering steam. Shortly after the publication of that paper, in the fall of 2003, Greenspan decided that fighting deflation wasn't enough. In his mind, what really needed defeating were plain, ordinary, everyday low prices. He decided that the country didn't have enough inflation, and so he set out to right that wrong. Greenspan explained his game plan on July 15, 2003, before the House Financial Services Committee. He determined that:

> …policy accommodation aimed at raising the growth of output, boosting the utilization of resources, and warding off unwelcome disinflation can be maintained for a considerable period without ultimately stoking inflationary pressures…. We face new challenges in maintaining price stability, specifically to prevent inflation from falling too low.

Low inflation was unwelcome in Greenspan's world, and he would see to it that we had more, rather than less, of it. The Chairman of the Fed, who couldn't spot a bubble or even define money, now, in addition to hand-picking the right interest rate for the country, was also going to decide on the appropriate level of inflation.

Compare Greenspan's viewpoint on inflation with that of legendary Fed chairman William McChesney Martin, who forcefully told the Senate on August 13, 1957, that "there is no validity whatever in the idea that any inflation, once accepted, can be confined to moderate proportions." It's hard to fathom how these two men could have actually held the same post.

Chapter 7

The Housing Hot Potato: The Real Estate Bubble Fuels the ATM

(2003–2007)

History repeats itself with the housing mania…a dangerous credit bubble brought on by financial innovations advocated by Greenspan creates irresponsible lending practices…real estate becomes the country's money pit.

By late 2003, the housing market was red hot. Yet the real jaw-dropping activity was not so much what was happening to the prices of homes but rather what was taking place when it came to financing them. What transpired at that time in the mortgage market was outlandish by historical standards, although relative to later developments it was somewhat pedestrian. Nonetheless, it's worth understanding the creative ways Americans were managing to buy houses that were more expensive than they could afford, because it illuminates the critical fact that the real estate mania was, in essence, a *credit bubble*.

Without the absurdly low level that lending standards fell to, the real estate market could never have developed into the bubble it ultimately became. Of course, were it not for the deregulation of the financial system, another cause championed by Alan Greenspan, and the securitization process that evolved from that deregulation, lending standards could never have dropped to the point where anyone who could fog a mirror could borrow almost any amount of money.

At the time, my business partner, John Ray Keil, and I couldn't understand how so many people were able to find such accommodating financing for their homes. John decided to figure out how this magic feat was performed. After he put the pieces of the puzzle together, we posted a three-part exposé on how the game was being played on our Web site in late November 2003.

We began the first installment, "The Housing Hot Potato: Part I," with a personal vignette written by John:

> My fascination with the housing market started with a ho-hum comment made by some friends at dinner. The couple we dined with were surprised that my wife and I didn't have a HELOC (home equity line of credit). After figuring out what a HELOC was (I had been too embarrassed to ask), I was shocked that they had mentioned it so matter-of-factly. I mean, very few people go around bragging about how much money they are borrowing on their credit cards. I had always thought of this couple as Middle America. The husband was a small-business owner and his wife a graphic designer. If *they* were using their HELOC like a credit card on steroids, what was the rest of America doing?

Around the same time, I developed a friendship with a mortgage broker who owned his own business. When I brought up John's conversation about the HELOC, he just chuckled and said, "You have no idea." I didn't. But the more I listened, the crazier the stories became. He told me about bad underwriting, fraudulent income documentation, and even 125s (which allowed owners to take out up to 125 percent of the equity they have in the home)—all of which were becoming almost standard operating procedure. The housing market was quickly becoming a dangerous game of hot potato, and the only ones who seemed to care was anyone left holding the hot potato—a mortgage about to default.

Everyone in the mortgage food chain—the home buyer, the mortgage broker, the home appraiser, and the lender—all stood to benefit as long as the buyer didn't default. One might have expected the lender, being the party at risk, to be the voice of reason. My partner, John, explained why that might not always be the case:

> [Lenders] face fierce competition from other lenders. Rather than make prudent, sound lending decisions, they rely on automated underwriting, and are often greatly influenced by the threat of losing market share. Lenders also rely on the upward slope of the average housing price in America. They assume that deals that go bad will eventually find a buyer without too much damage done to principal. But this will not be the case should housing prices flatten or fall. [Author's note: In that case lenders would be stuck with a bad mortgage—that is, a hot potato—which is what began to happen en masse in late 2007.] Lenders are intent on growing, no matter what the costs.

As long as housing prices rose there were few hot potatoes, as a homeowner could always refinance. Consequently, lenders kept getting more aggressive and so did home buyers; naturally, that phenomenon kept housing prices climbing, which kept the whole game going. The Fed did its part by keeping interest rates too low.

On February 23, 2004, Greenspan gave a speech titled "Understanding Household Debt Obligations" in which he told homeowners that they had been acting too conservatively and it was costing them money:

> One way homeowners attempt to manage their payment risk is to use fixed-rate mortgages, which typically allow homeowners to prepay their debt when interest rates fall but do not involve an increase in payments when interest rates rise.... Indeed, recent research within the Federal Reserve suggests that many homeowners might have saved tens of thousands of dollars had they held adjustable-rate mortgages, rather than fixed-rate mortgages during the past decade....

He reiterated the point for all the slow learners.

> To the degree that households are driven by fears of payment shocks but are willing to manage their own interest rate risks, *the traditional fixed-rate mortgage may be an expensive way of financing a home.*" [italics mine]

Leaving no potential source of trouble out of the mix, he also invited the mortgage industry to get with the program: "*American consumers might benefit if lenders provided greater mortgage product alternatives to the traditional fixed-rate mortgage.*" [italics mine]

Greenspan was extolling the virtues of floating-rate mortgages when interest rates were at the lowest level they had been in over 50 years. Almost anyone who took that advice from the man who was in charge of setting interest rates for our country can not be happy with what has happened since he dispensed it. In the two years that followed that statement, Greenspan more than quadrupled interest rates in a series of 17 hikes, from 1 percent to 4.5 percent. (On the other hand, anyone who did the opposite of what he suggested and took out a fixed-rate mortgage saw no impact on the cost of financing his or her home from those rate hikes.) However, due to *innovations* on the part of the mortgage industry—like negative amortization adjustable-rate mortgages (aka option arms), no-document and stated income loans—the pain from those hikes was postponed and the real estate market kept soaring even as rates rose.

The year 2004 was to the housing bubble what 1998 was to the 1990s' stock market bubble: the moment in time when participants started to feel truly invincible and behaved accordingly. During that phase, in both the stock market and real estate bubbles, imagination was king. In the case of the stock market, back in 1998, disbelief was suspended for stocks generically, but blindly so for anything related to technology. In the real estate bubble, it was assumed that not only would prices continue to get higher indefinitely but literally *any* financing scheme would not be turned down. Because prices kept rising for homes, along with interest rates, the dollar volume of different creative forms of nontraditional financing—like subprime and Alt-A mortgages—began to explode. (Alt-As are nonprime mortgages catering to those wanting large mortgages without standard documentation—many required little documentation and were often referred to as *liar's loans.*)

As you can see in Figure 9, subprime borrowing accounted for a whopping 20 percent or more of the total mortgage lending for 2004 to 2006. In 1997, by comparison, they accounted for less than 3 percent of all mortgages. And as Figure 10 makes clear, the volume of Alt-As also saw large increases while home equity loans

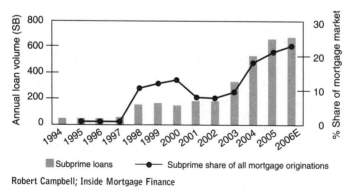

Robert Campbell; Inside Mortgage Finance

Figure 9 Primed for Disaster

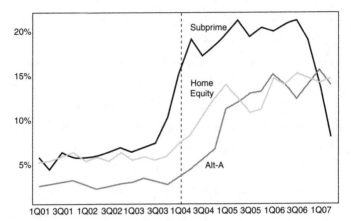

Goldman Sachs; Inside Mortgage Finance

Figure 10 What Happened in 2004?

Sales of "affordability products"—subprime, Alt-A, home equity loans—as a proportion of total mortgage originations spiked at the start of 2004.

grew almost as fast. To put the fury that was the mortgage market at that time into perspective, from 2003 to 2005 outstanding mortgage debt *grew* by $3.7 trillion—an amount almost equal to the $3.8 trillion of total outstanding mortgage debt as of 1990. In three years the country accumulated what had previously taken over two hundred years to rack up.

One might wonder how the Chairman felt with the mortgage-for-anyone-with-a-pulse music blasting away. Was he concerned? Was he worried that some of these subprime borrowers might get into trouble, or that some of the lenders might be acting foolishly? On April 8,

2005, in his speech "Consumer Finance," Greenspan let the country know where he stood:

> [T]echnological advances have resulted in increased efficiency and scale within the financial services industry. Innovation has brought about a multitude of new products, such as subprime loans and niche credit programs for immigrants.... With these advances in technology, lenders have taken advantage of credit-scoring models and other techniques for efficiently extending credit to a broader spectrum of consumers.... These improvements have led to rapid growth in subprime mortgage lending; indeed, today subprime mortgages account for roughly 10 percent [Author's note: that figure was a bit low] of the number of all mortgages outstanding, up from just 1 or 2 percent in the early 1990s.

Translation? Technology allowed lending institutions to offer products to people who couldn't get loans before, and the volumes of those new creative loans grew dramatically. Applying technology to lending money resulted in massive numbers of homeowners getting more money than they could afford to repay. Once again the Chairman championed a cause that encouraged the public to behave in a way that most would come to regret. Greenspan seemed to feel that generically extending more credit to more people was a benefit to all: "As we reflect on the evolution of consumer credit in the United States, we must conclude that innovation and structural change in the financial services industry have been critical in providing expanded access to credit for the vast majority of consumers."

In fact, it was as if Greenspan believed that extending credit in larger amounts to more people was *such* an unadulterated positive development that he wanted *his* share of the credit: "This fact underscores the importance of *our roles as policymakers*, researchers, bankers, and consumer advocates in fostering constructive innovation that is both responsive to market demand and *beneficial* to consumers." [italics mine]

As was often the case with the Chairman, he didn't have a good grasp of what was taking place. In a *60 Minutes* interview with Leslie Stahl on September 16, 2007, Greenspan claimed he knew about the questionable subprime lending tactics that gave loans to home buyers with low adjustable interest rates that could rise precipitously. At the time, however, he didn't understand the severe economic consequences they posed: "While I was aware a lot of these practices were going on, I had no notion of how significant they had become until very late. *I really didn't get it until very late in 2005 and 2006.*" [italics mine]

Whether Greenspan even understood it then we won't know until the FOMC transcripts for that time frame are released in a few years. But it's clear he certainly didn't comprehend the potential damage of an unfettered expansion of credit when he was extolling its virtues in the spring of 2005.

Someone who was not sanguine about the developments *he* saw taking place in the real estate market was Greenspan's predecessor, Paul Volcker. Volcker published an editorial in the *Washington Post* on April 10, 2005, called "An Economy on Thin Ice." In it, he discussed several "disturbing trends" he saw, one of which was occurring in the real estate market:

> We sit here absorbed in a debate about how to maintain Social Security—and, more important, Medicare—when the baby boomers retire. But right now, those same boomers are spending like there's no tomorrow. If we can believe the numbers, personal savings in the United States have practically disappeared.... We are buying a lot of housing at rising prices, but home ownership has become a vehicle for *borrowing* as much as a source of financial security. [italics mine]

Volcker had described the housing ATM, though in more polite terms.

With four months to go in his final term, Greenspan gave a speech on September 28, 2005, titled "Economic

Flexibility," where he attempted to set the record straight on what he had accomplished as Fed Chairman—essentially an attempt to absolve himself of any blame for our twin bubbles. While we've already covered much of Greenspan's backtracking, he did make some new and interesting claims.

The Chairman began his bubble defense with the conclusion he hoped we would arrive at: "Relying on policymakers to perceive when speculative asset bubbles have developed and then to implement timely policies to address successfully these misalignments in asset prices is simply not realistic."

Here he is making two claims. The first is that one can't perceive when a bubble is occurring. We already know this statement to be false. Many people saw the 1990s' stock bubble for what it was; in fact, rather than being difficult to *perceive*, they found it virtually impossible to *ignore*. Ditto for the real estate bubble. As for Greenspan's second claim, that policy options can't be implemented to arrest a bubble, that is also untrue. What would be correct to say is that one can't know in advance exactly what action might be required to stop a bubble. One thing we do know for sure, though, is that Greenspan never really tried.

The Chairman continued: "As the Federal Open Market Committee (FOMC) transcripts of the mid-1990s duly note, we at the Fed were uncomfortable with a stock market that appeared as early as 1996 to disconnect from its moorings." In this book, we've reviewed those transcripts. They reveal that while there was some discussion about a bubble in 1994 and briefly in 1996, the stock market bubble was *not* a focus of discussion at the FOMC meetings, as Greenspan implies.

The truth is somewhat different from what Greenspan contended in his speech; he didn't see the bubble because he was mesmerized by the concept of a technologically driven productivity miracle.

Greenspan then tried again to convince the world that he had attempted to fight the stock market bubble (that he never saw):

> Yet the significant monetary tightening of 1994 did not prevent what must by then have been the beginnings of the bubble of the 1990s. And equity prices continued to rise during the tightening of policy between mid-1999 and May 2000. Indeed, the equity market's ability to withstand periods of tightening arguably *reinforced* the bull market's momentum. [italics mine]

We have seen that it wasn't his minor bouts of tightening that were the reason for the bubble's growth, as he claimed here; rather, its reinforcement came from him constantly setting interest rates at a level that was too low and holding them there for far too long. His continual cheerleading regarding the magic of technology and productivity that so captivated him encouraged others to tumble to similarly wrongheaded economic and invest-ment decisions, ultimately making matters worse. After all, he was the Fed Chairman; he was *supposed* to know these things.

The Chairman made a new admission: "The FOMC knew that tools were available to choke off the stock market boom, but those tools would only have been effective if they undermined market participants' confidence in future stability." He is exactly correct. To defuse a bubble, market participants must have a regard for risk. It is not clear what tools he is referring to here, as a discussion of these tools was not a regular feature of FOMC meetings. Presumably he must have meant changing margin requirements, a tactic at other times he has said would not work, despite the fact that commodity exchanges utilize exactly that tactic as they deem it necessary. He pressed on in this vein: "Market participants, however, read the resilience of the economy and stock prices in the face of monetary tightening as an indication of undiscounted market strength." He continued: "By the late 1990s, it appeared to us that very aggressive action would have been required to counteract the euphoria that developed in the wake of extraordinary gains in productivity growth spawned by technological change." While technology and productivity gains were what captivated the Chairman, it was his policies that were primarily responsible for the euphoria, not technology or productivity—they were just rationalizations.

As for his statement "it appeared to us that very aggressive action would have been required," that is an interesting observation on Greenspan's part, because what might be required to fight the bubble was not a topic of conversation at FOMC meetings in the late 1990s.

Then came the coup de grâce: Greenspan would have us believe that had he fought the bubble that he didn't recognize, a draconian outcome was preordained: "In short, we would have needed to risk precipitating a significant recession, with unknown consequences." Though he makes it sound as though serious bubble-fighting sessions took place, the record shows they did not. Regardless, it was not guaranteed that if Greenspan had fought the bubble the United States would have had a recession. Greenspan was correct when he said the Fed does have tools, even if he never used them. It may have been possible for a prudent man to have defeated the bubble short of precipitating a recession, but since we had one anyway when the bubble burst, fighting it wouldn't have left us *worse* off. Quite the contrary. Risking a recession in an attempt to stop the bubble would have been a good policy decision, because the longer bubbles expand, the more damage they do when they burst. It's worth bearing in mind that the bursting of the equity bubble would have done even more damage than it did had a new real estate bubble not followed. (That subsequent bubble, however, has only served to postpone the inevitable and guarantee an outcome that will be far worse.)

Greenspan wound up his defense: "The alternative was to wait for the eventual exhaustion of the forces of the boom. We concluded that the latter course was by far the safer." Again, he suggests that discussions took place at FOMC meetings regarding whether it was better to fight a bubble or clean up the mess afterward. The transcripts show that they did not. Greenspan did muddy the waters on this subject a bit by telling Congress in June 1999 that "it is the job of economic policy makers to mitigate the fallout when it occurs, and, hopefully, ease the transition to the next expansion." However the "fallout" he was referring to was the ending of an economic expansion, not the stock market bubble. What Greenspan also failed to comprehend is that even if he and the FOMC members had seriously discussed the stock market bubble and concluded that it would be *safer* to deal with the aftermath than try to put a stop to it, as he claims they did, it would have been a terrible decision. It is a variation of a bailout, and ends up causing people to take more risk than they should because they feel that they will not get hurt. The term for that outcome is *moral hazard*.

Mervyn King, governor of the Bank of England, on September 12, 2007, described the dangers of such policies, wherever they might occur: "The provision of such liquidity support undermines the efficient pricing of risk …that encourages excessive risk-taking and sows the seeds of a future financial crisis." This was precisely the policy Greenspan pursued in the 1990s. (Unfortunately, when King faced an issue of moral hazard just days after making that statesmanlike comment, he caved in to pressure and guaranteed all depositors at Britain's troubled mortgage lender Northern Rock.)

Jeremy Grantham, Chairman of GMO, in his October 2007 monthly letter, brilliantly and eloquently summed up the Fed's propensity under Greenspan to encourage excessive risk-taking and what that led to:

> As you can see, they [the Fed] have made no secret about it. To let bubbles form unimpeded and yet to move to cushion the subsequent decline is a simple and workable definition of moral hazard. The fact that they define it as not moving to prop up asset prices, but only to cushion the economic effects of asset prices declining, is sophistry. It amounts to exactly the same thing. In contrast, The Bank of England, my former semi-heroes, have long maintained that it is appropriate for central bankers to be concerned with asset bubbles, knowing as we surely must by now how destabilizing they can be.
>
> Recognizing bubbles is held to be hard: "To spot a bubble in advance," said Greenspan, "requires a judgment that hundreds of thousands of investors had it all wrong." Greenspan has since contradicted this ridiculous comment many times when describing investor herding and irrational behavioral markets. And his great 2000 bubble, partly indeed his

creation, peaked 65 percent higher than any previous market. Not only did it look like a Himalayan peak, but statistically it was a 3-standard deviation, 100-year event. Far from being hard to spot, it was impossible to miss. The current housing bubble was also easy to see. The seeing part is easy, but acting is not.

Unfortunately for Greenspan, even the "seeing part" wasn't easy.

In later years, the Chairman appeared comfortable discussing the equity bubble, even calling it by its name, because he probably felt that it was ancient history and the country had enjoyed a happy (if temporary) ending in any case. After all, the economy had recovered, as had the stock market, and thus all was well. But he had merely replaced one bubble with a new one, as Figure 11 makes clear.

Figure 11 reveals that the median price of a home divided by the median income in the country rocketed to a level that was also 3-standard deviations from historic norms. This means if prices were to revert to normal levels, which they tend to do, they would have to drop 25 percent immediately or stay flat for five years.

At its heart, the real estate bubble was a debt bubble, in which as long as the collateral was a house, it seemed that anyone could borrow almost as much money as he or she wanted. As mentioned earlier, one of the impor-

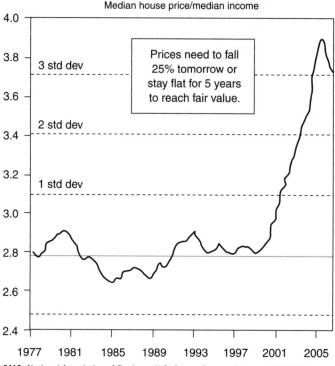

Median house price/median income

Prices need to fall 25% tomorrow or stay flat for 5 years to reach fair value.

3 std dev

2 std dev

1 std dev

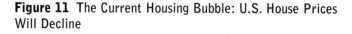

GMO; National Association of Realtors; U.S. Census Bureau. Data as of 7/31/07.

Figure 11 The Current Housing Bubble: U.S. House Prices Will Decline

tant features of the real estate bubble was the fact that homeowners routinely extracted some portion of the equity that was created as the price of homes soared, and they spent it. The official name for that process is *mortgage-equity withdrawal* (MEW).

As Figure 12 illustrates, the amount of money extracted from homes in the post–stock market bubble economic recovery was staggering; it totally dwarfs what occurred in the past. Mortgage-equity withdrawal, or the *housing ATM*, as I began calling it in May 2004, occurred on such a mammoth scale that it alone was responsible for a large portion of GDP growth over this period. As can be seen in Figure 13, without the money taken from the housing ATM, GDP growth would have been much less than half of what it was reported to be. The chart also makes clear how abnormal home-equity withdrawal was in the post–stock market bubble economic recovery compared to those of the past and that without it, the economic growth from 2001 to 2007 would barely have registered as an economic expansion by historic stan-

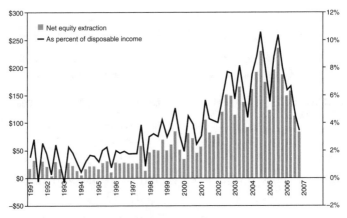

www.contraryinvestor.com; Kennedy-Greenspan

Figure 12 Mortgage-Equity Withdrawal, Billions of Dollars, Quarterly, Kennedy-Greenspan

Mortgage-equity withdrawals = my house is my own ATM machine.

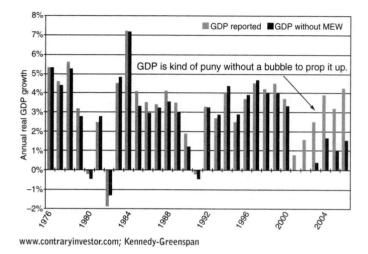

www.contraryinvestor.com; Kennedy-Greenspan

Figure 13 GDP and Mortgage-Equity Withdrawal

dards. This phenomenon also helps explain why job creation in this economic cycle has been so much weaker than those of the past. If one takes into consideration that approximately 40 percent of all jobs created in this economic expansion were real estate related[1] (for example, construction workers, real-estate agents, appraisers, mortgage processors), it is clear that for all intents and purposes, real estate *was* the economy after the stock market bubble burst in 2000.

Figure 14 demonstrates that while the country has experienced frothy real estate markets in the past, nothing has even come close to rivaling what transpired from 2000 to 2006.

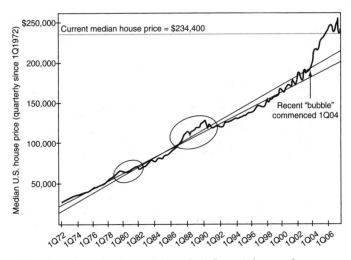

Goldman Sachs Research estimates; Goldman Sachs Economic forecasts; Census Bureau

Figure 14 The Incomparable Real Estate Bubble of 2000–2006

National house prices relative to the long-term trend line.

One can also see the impact of the housing bubble in the debt statistics, since after all, it was debt that drove the real estate market. While there is no magic number that guarantees a financial accident, Figure 15 certainly illustrates how extraordinarily high household debt as a percentage of GDP had become. It is staggering to contemplate the fact that total mortgage debt outstanding of $13.3 trillion at the end of 2006 was more than double the $6.2 trillion it had been at the end of 1999. That is an alarming increase in debt compared to GDP, which

www.contraryinvestor.com

Figure 15 Household Debt as Percentage of GDP

only grew from $9.3 trillion to $13.2 trillion over the same period.

The speculation in real estate by the public and the associated mountain of real estate debt that this new bubble spawned posed a serious risk to the U.S. Robert Campbell, of "The Campbell Real Estate Timing Letter," addressed this ticking time bomb in the September 2007 issue of his newsletter.

Driven by the ultra-low interest rates and ultra-easy credit that was extended to unqualified homebuyers, Greenspan's monetary policies led to a massive bubble in U.S. housing prices that had no real

underlying support. But guess what? When prices
stop rising—as they always do—reality sets in, the
market blows up, and housing prices fall. Why?
Because borrowers now face the fact that they do
not have—nor did they ever have—enough income
to make payments on all the housing debt they
were so eager to take on.

It wasn't just homeowners who piled on debt; corporations did as well. Figure 16 makes clear that the total
debt outstanding in the United States expressed as a percentage of GDP, a measure of overall leverage for the
American economy, continued to ratchet higher.

More ominously, the number of dollars of debt required
to grow GDP by a dollar grew at 10 percent per year dur-

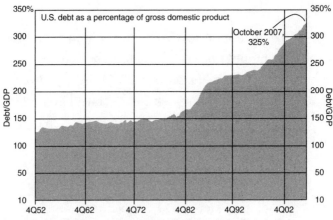

Grant's Interest Rat Observer, Federal Reserve, Bureau of Economic Analysis

Figure 16 Much Borrowing, Little Growth

ing the real estate–driven expansion. In other words, it took continually higher amounts of leverage to generate the same dollar of economic output. As Figure 17 illustrates, in this economic cycle, the rate of debt growth versus GDP growth is almost two and a half times what the United States experienced in the prior expansion.

Only the debt-driven takeover binge of the late 1980s, which ended with the collapse of the savings and loan industry, comes close. Yet the growth rate of debt to GDP in the cycle illustrated in Figure 17 was 50 percent higher than that previous one. It's worth noting that the use of debt to boost growth barely moved the needle in past economic recoveries, before Greenspan became the Chairman.

Financial innovation and euphoria induced by the real estate bubble led to the debt creation just discussed,

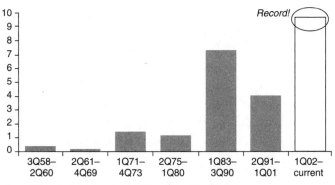

Gloom, Boom, & Doom Report; David Rosenberg, Merrill Lynch

Figure 17 The Most Pronounced Debt Cycle Ever

The chart shows the total economy debt-to-GDP ratio for business cycles since 1958.

and it is the real estate market that will create the hangover we will all experience over the next several years. The pain will be in proportion to the size of the revelry that preceded it. So, just how big was the party? It is difficult to illustrate the national real estate market and the wild lending practices that supported it with just one example. Nevertheless, if we look at the prices of housing stocks, admittedly a poor proxy for home prices, but a wonderful barometer with which to ascertain the pace of speculative activity, we can get a sense of how out of control the bash was. Figure 18 compares the stock price action of a basket of publicly traded housing stocks from 2000 to 2007 to a basket of Internet stocks from 1995 to 2002.

Looking at Figure 18, it is clear that the madness in the housing bubble was similar to what we saw with Internet stocks, the epicenter of speculation in the previous stock bubble. However, there is one enormous difference between the two bubbles. The 2000–2007 real estate bubble was fueled by debt whereas the previous stock market bubble wasn't. So, the hangover is likely to be far more severe from the real estate bubble as it unwinds. How big might the hangover be? Robert Campbell, in his November 15, 2007, report, attempted to describe the problem:

From 2004 to 2007, banks and mortgage companies were making trillions of dollars of ultra-liberal

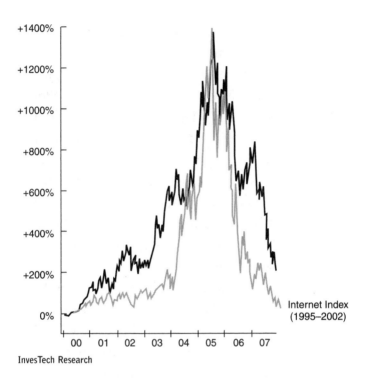

InvesTech Research

Figure 18 Housing Bubble Bellwether Index

This chart can easily be anointed "The Greenspan Mountain Range."

adjustable rate mortgage loans to millions upon millions of Americans who had little or no chance of making payments on those loans to maturity. Counting on rising real estate prices to solve this problem, it effectively turned the U.S. housing market into a system of Ponzi finance, where new debt was needed to service the old. Like all Ponzi schemes, it was doomed from the start. When prices stopped rising—

as they always do—it has led to a *credit crunch* and an inevitable housing market bust.

The housing market is coming to terms with the fact that homes are not worth what people paid for them. This verdict is being rendered loud and clear all over the country: 45 out of 50 states are now reporting rising foreclosure rates, according to RealtyTrac. Not surprisingly, this has resulted in a record tightening in lending standards. In August 2007, residential mortgages were harder to get than in any time of the 17-year history of a Fed banking survey of senior loan officers.

Truth is, the banking write downs could easily be greater than $400 billion. As I see it, and based on the fact that trillions of dollars of ultra-easy ARM loans were made during the boom years, a high percentage of these loans are almost guaranteed to go into foreclosure for all of the following reasons:

1. ARM payments are resetting higher by 50% to 100%;
2. Lending standards are tightening;
3. Falling prices have made homes worth less than their underlying loans;
4. American consumers have a record debt-to-income ratio;
5. America's savings rate is at record low;
6. A recession is on the horizon.

Adding all this up, it is not inconceivable that total banking losses could approach $1 trillion before this housing bust is over. It is quite easy to see that we will all be paying an enormous price for the decisions Alan Greenspan made as Chairman of the Federal Reserve.

Conclusion

The Consequences of the Loss of Fear

(2007 and Beyond)

Greenspan bailed out the world's largest equity bubble with the world's largest real estate bubble. That combination easily equates to the biggest orgy of speculation and debt creation the United States (and the world) has ever seen. Unfortunately, Greenspan's legacy will not just be those two bubbles, their attendant busts, and the trillions of dollars of debt left in their wake. Operation Enduring Bubble—what I call Greenspan's monetary and interest rate decisions that created the real estate bubble—also exacted a heavy toll on the dollar.

From the end of 2001, when the bulk of post–stock market bubble rate cuts had largely ended, until Greenspan left office in January 2006, the U.S. dollar declined in value by roughly 24 percent versus the basket of foreign currencies known as the *dollar index*. Compared to the currency of our Canadian neighbors, the U.S. dollar did even worse, declining by 28 percent over the same time period. What this means is that Greenspan's policies, in those five years alone, contributed to reducing the net worth of every U.S. citizen by 28 percent in comparison with a Canadian of equal financial means in terms of what his money would buy for him. Versus the rest of the world, the U.S. currency declined in value because of policies Greenspan pursued that caused investors worldwide to feel that the U.S. dollar was less attractive to hold than other currencies. In short, the vote across the globe has been one of little confidence. Even currencies that were at one time derided, such as the Mexican peso, Russian ruble, and Brazilian dollar, have strengthened considerably over this time frame against the U.S. dollar.

The eyes of U.S. citizens tend to glaze over when the topic of the U.S. dollar's value in the foreign exchange market is raised. The United States has been spoiled; the U.S. dollar has been the world's reserve currency for almost a hundred years. Today that status is threatened as a result of Greenspan's dual bubbles. If the United States continues on its current path, the U.S. dollar will be chronically weak, and it is a virtual certainty that it will no longer be the world's sole reserve currency. Many U.S. citizens feel that the value of the dollar is of no consequence to them except when they vacation outside of the United States. The actual loss of wealth that I describe leaves folks of that mindset unperturbed. The Chairman is one of those people in the unconcerned camp.

Greenspan told attendees at the Learning Annex Wealth Expo conference on November 18, 2007, that "so long as the dollar weakness does not create inflation … then I think it's a market phenomenon, which aside from those who travel the world, has no real fundamental economic consequences." It is difficult to put into perspective how shockingly naive that comment is, coming from the man formerly in charge of the organization whose name is on every bill in your wallet. First of all, a decline in the dollar is nearly always inflationary. As the cost of imports rises, domestic competitors raise prices accordingly. But to say that the decline in the dollar has had no real consequences is just plain incorrect.

Take just one example: oil. From the end of 2001 until the end of 2007, a barrel of oil has risen in price from roughly $20 to $100, a fivefold increase. But someone who lived in Europe during that same time period has seen the price rise from 22 euros to only 68 euros, essentially a threefold increase. So, the price for a European at the end of 2007 was only two-thirds that of an American. Since it is nearly impossible to name any consumer good that can be produced anywhere in the world without energy, it's easy to see the ripple effect of the weak dollar with this one (albeit very important) commodity. Similar examples exist in virtually everything, though perhaps to a lesser extent. That the former Chairman of the Federal Reserve could hold the viewpoint that Greenspan espoused in November 2007 is nearly incomprehensible to me, but there it is for the world to see.

The U.S. dollar has weakened even further, and in some cases dramatically so, since the time the Chairman left office at the beginning of 2006. One important reason for the continued weakness has been the negative reaction by investors worldwide to the sorry state of affairs that Greenspan left his successor, Ben Bernanke. (This is not to relieve Bernanke of accountability for his decisions; it simply acknowledges that the problems the new Fed chief faced were preexisting. In my view, the two of them are birds of a feather and their decisions on most matters would likely be similar.)

Bernanke's predicament was caused by the fragility of the financial system, itself a consequence of the cumulative effect of Greenspan's decisions as Fed chief. That brittleness can best be illustrated by the fact that on August 19, 2007, with the Dow Jones Industrial Average just 8 percent lower than its *prior month's all-time high of 14,000*, the Federal Reserve found it necessary to hold an unscheduled meeting and cut the discount rate (not the federal funds rate) 50 basis points. The rationalization for that desperate measure was the fact that the U.S. financial system—and that of much of the world—was swimming in several hundred billion, if not trillions, of dollars of *securitized* mortgage paper that had become illiquid. Those mortgage assets had largely become illiquid because no institution wanted to sell whatever problem mortgage paper they held for what it would fetch in the marketplace, as that might result in a substantial loss.

Many of those mortgage "assets" were of the subprime variety, and a large chunk of them weren't just illiquid but worthless. Nonetheless, the Fed had stepped into the fray and would follow up that surprise discount rate cut with two more interest rate cuts over the next two months.

To appreciate how far we've traveled thanks to Greenspan in terms of the amount of stock market pain required to obtain a helping hand from the Fed, note that in October 1987, when the Fed abandoned its previous tightening policy and slashed interest rates, the Dow Jones Industrial Average had fallen nearly 40 percent from its highs of that summer. Quite a contrast to the minuscule amount of damage inflicted on stock prices in August 2007 when the Fed sprang into action. Of course in 1987, Greenspan had only recently taken over from Paul Volcker, a man who worried about the soundness of the U.S. currency and financial system above all else. Therefore, stock market participants had not yet come to expect the Fed to protect them from losses.

Under Greenspan's reign, however, the U.S. financial system came to depend on assistance from the Fed whenever it had taken on too much risk, and fall 2007 was another such occasion. Rather than take a loss, financial institutions wanted to be bailed out. Financial deregulation, a process routinely championed by Greenspan, had helped to create this predicament. So had the Chairman himself, when he specifically suggested to homeowners that they take out adjustable-rate mortgages in 2004, just months before the Fed was set to raise interest rates 17 times over the next two years.

During Greenspan's tenure, the creative destruction component of capitalism was routinely suppressed. The main consequence of this suppression was a loss of fear. Thus, the normal risk reduction response to periodic financial pain never occurred, as Greenspan wouldn't even allow small crises to run their course. Instead, as people lost respect for the idea that they might lose money, risk taking continually escalated until the situation reached the point where it is now: the United States, individually and collectively, is swimming in an ocean of debt that has been rapidly ratcheting higher. At the same time, the country is experiencing a declining real estate market that supports much of that debt, a sinking economy that has been dependent on an unsustainable real estate bubble, and a weak currency. Plus, there are over $500 trillion worth of derivatives that Warren Buffett has described as "financial instruments of mass destruction." You couldn't have created a more precarious environment if you had tried.

Naturally, that's not how Greenspan sees it. As if to add insult to injury, on November 24, 2007, Greenspan proclaimed to an audience in Oslo, Norway, that he had no role in the housing bubble: "Markets are becoming aware of the fact that the decline in housing is not stopping.... *I have no particular regrets.* [italics mine] The housing bubble is not a reflection of what we did, as it is a global phenomenon." Earlier the Chairman, as noted in Chapter 6, claimed that the United States couldn't have a housing bubble because (among other reasons) real estate was a local market. He would now have us believe that the global dimension of the housing bubbles "proved" he was not to blame. His argument is illogical and inaccurate...but classic Greenspan.

Viewing his own "accomplishments" through rose-colored glasses obfuscates the harsh reality we are all forced to live with now. Yet, Greenspan's major short-coming—and critical flaw—was not his mistakes but his *refusal to admit them.* Thus, he never learned from his errors in judgment, repeating them time and again over the course of 19 years.

The financial world Greenspan has left behind will be a treacherous one to navigate that will leave many wounded in its wake. There is no debate: Greenspan was no "Maestro;" he was the master of the United States' descent into financial turmoil. The evidence speaks for itself.

NOTES

Introduction

1. Unless otherwise noted, when I refer to *interest rates*, I mean the federal funds rate, which is the one the FOMC targets.

2. The word *bubble* as it pertains to investments has many connotations and definitions. My favorite example can be found on page 96. Determining that a bubble exists is somewhat subjective, though not terribly difficult. No objective definition exists, though Jeremy Grantham, Chairman of GMO, a global investment management firm, believes that bubbles are definable events where the price action is two standard deviations from a long-term trend. Based on his definition, Grantham's research found that the U.S. stock market and real estate bubbles were the twenty-eighth and twenty-ninth bubbles, respectively, in financial history, with the Dutch tulip craze being the first.

3. FOMC = Federal Open Market Committee. The Fed's Web site defines it as the monetary policymaking body of the Federal Reserve System. It is respon-

sible for formulation of a monetary policy designed to promote growth, full employment, stable prices, and a sustainable pattern of international trade and payments. Martin Mayer, in his book *The Fed* [pp. 143–144], describes the FOMC's role as follows:

> The hands on the wheel are those of the Open Market Committee, who decide when and how to buy or sell paper for the Fed's portfolio, increasing (when they buy) or decreasing (when they sell) the reserves of the banking system and thus the money supply of the country—reducing (when they buy) or raising (when they sell) the interest rates the banks will pay for funds and charge for loans.

In other, simpler words, the Fed increases liquidity, thereby lowering interest rates, or it decreases liquidity, causing rates to rise. The former is known as *easing credit* or *easy money*. The latter is called *tightening* or *tight money*. Also, while the Fed "prints" money via its operations, it doesn't actually turn the crank on the paper stuff that is spent. The Treasury makes that money.

4. When I refer to the *stock market*, I am refering to the Standard & Poor's 500 Index.

5. I've lightly edited my prior columns to make them more readable in the context of this book.

6. Transcripts of FOMC meetings are available for all to see on the Federal Reserve Board's Web site, www.federalreserve.gov/FOMC/Transcripts. The FOMC provides the complete transcripts for the entire year with a five-year lag.

Chapter 1

1. Stephen Pizzo, et al., *Inside Job: The Looting of America's Savings and Loans*, McGraw-Hill, New York, 1989, p. 266.

2. The *Greenspan Put* is the belief by market participants that in times of stock market distress Greenspan was willing to increase liquidity by whatever level necessary to keep the stock market from declining in any meaningful way. A perfect definition of which can be found on page 62.

3. A *margin requirement* is the minimum amount of money that can be deposited in order to be allowed to trade a financial instrument. For stocks, it is 50 percent of the value of the amount purchased. When margin requirements are raised, it takes more money to control the same size stock purchase, and vice versa.

Chapter 2

1. "Irrational exuberance" was a phrase Greenspan used in a speech given at the American Enterprise Institute on December 5, 1996. "Clearly, sustained low

inflation implies less uncertainty about the future, and lower risk premiums imply higher prices of stocks and other earning assets. We can see that in the inverse relationship exhibited by price/earnings ratios and the rate of inflation in the past. But how do we know when irrational exuberance has unduly escalated asset values, which then become subject to unexpected and prolonged contractions as they have in Japan over the past decade?" At the time of the speech it was interpreted to mean that the Chairman was concerned about a frothy stock market. But it quickly became clear that even if he was worried, he didn't intend to do anything about it. And of course it soon became clearer still that he was not worried at all.

Chapter 3

1. Alan Greenspan, *The Age of Turbulence: Adventures in a New World,* Penguin, 2007, p. 179.
2. Speech to the New York group of The Investment Bankers Association of America on October 19, 1955.
3. Shaw was a hedge fund that had gotten into trouble.

Chapter 4

1. Y2K was the so-called *millennium bug.* There was concern that computer chips might malfunction when their internal clocks had to deal with the year

2000. The fear of the potential consequence of such an outcome caused most individual organizations to replace important electronic devices. The Fed dealt with it by massively increasing liquidity in the fourth quarter of 1999.

2. *Bubbleonians* is a term I began using in October 1999 to describe those people who were participating in the bubble and who seemed to feel that we were in a perpetual bull market.

3. Fred Hickey, *High Tech Strategist* (newsletter), December 1999.

4. Marc Faber, *Gloom, Boom & Doom Report*, August 2000, www.gloomboomdoom.com.

Chapter 5

1. American Enterprise Institute, *Economic Outlook*, November 9, 2000.

2. Security analysts are finance professionals who make buy, sell, and hold recommendations based on their research into various industries and companies.

Chapter 6

1. Sheila Muto, "C'mon, My House Is Worth More Than That," *Wall Street Journal*, August 20, 2002.

Chapter 7

1. *Grant's Interest Rate Observer*, April 21, 2006. "We will quote once more an amazing nugget of research

from Asha Bangalore, economist at Northern Trust Co.: No less than 40 percent of new jobs since 2001 owe their existence, directly or indirectly, to the real-estate levitation."